TALES FROM THE MINNESOTA SPORTS BEAT

TALES FROM THE MINNESOTA SPORTS BEAT

◆

A LIFETIME ON DEADLINE

PATRICK REUSSE

WITH CHIP SCOGGINS

FOREWORD BY DAN BARREIRO

MINNESOTA
HISTORICAL
SOCIETY PRESS

mnhspress.org

The Minnesota Historical Society Press is a member of the Association of University Presses.

Manufactured in the United States of America

10 9 8 7 6 5 4 3 2

♾ The paper used in this publication meets the minimum requirements of the American National Standard for Information Sciences—Permanence for Printed Library Materials, ANSI Z39.48–1984.

Front cover photo by Jerry Holt, courtesy of the *Star Tribune*

International Standard Book Number
ISBN: 978-1-68134-230-6 (paper)
ISBN: 978-1-68134-231-3 (e-book)

Library of Congress Control Number: 2022933904

This and other Minnesota Historical Society Press books are available from popular e-book vendors.

In memory of Mike Augustin (1940–1997)

Grand Friend. Superb Colleague. Respected Competitor.

And in gratitude to scores more Minnesota sports media members over the past six decades who fit into those categories.

CONTENTS

FOREWORD

DAN BARREIRO

By all rights, I should back in. I should bury the lede, as folks say in the newspaper business. I should make you search high and most probably low for the "nut graf," the paragraph that is supposed to distill the essence of the story, spell out what it's all about.

Good luck if you expect to find it before the jump.

Patrick Reusse, you see, has made a mockery of the time-honored daily newspaper tradition that demands you get to where you're supposed to go real fast.

Patrick gets there when he gets there, not a paragraph sooner.

And that's the beauty of it.

I call it the Reusse Rule: Have enough faith in your own ability to fashion a story and the readers' willingness to trust you to take them there. (OK, maybe there is some stubbornness sprinkled in there too.) The trust is built over not days or weeks, even months or years, but over decades, and thousands of columns.

I haven't run any of these Reusse Rules by Patrick. But I've watched him write for a long time. I've gone over to the Dark Side—full-time talk radio for the past 17 years—but before that, I sat side by side with him in crowded press boxes, both of us dodging double-barreled Sid attacks, celebrating Game 7 World Series victories at the Metrodome, savaging incomprehensible Vikings losses in the same building, the reliable, Radio Shack flip-top computer our instrument of exhilaration or obliteration.

< ix >

I've read him long enough to believe that these are the rules that have guided him to that rarefied air that few columnists reach: Institution.

I don't mean the kind of institution who gets a statue. The man himself, who cannot abide grandiosity, would probably take a ball-peen hammer to it. I mean the kind who has gained an unusual measure of respect, especially among his peers, for his writing presence and the power of his personality. And because he has a gift.

As trite as it reads, Reusse is doing what he was put on this earth to do.

Write.

Write columns.

Make people mad. Make 'em wonder. Make them smile.

Put people on a pedestal who otherwise would never get there. Take the feet out from others who have looked down from that same pedestal for too long, and too easily.

Tell stories. Tell people off. And bank on the equity in his back pocket to do it: born here, grew up here, always lived here. Cutting Minnesota icons to size is always more acceptable from One of Us. I've lived here for 35 years, which is 23 years longer than I've lived anyplace else in the world, including my hometown of Gary, Indiana. Doesn't matter: I'm still not one of us. Even now on the radio, when I rip a Minnesota team or athlete or institution, the reply occasionally is *What do you know? Go back to Gary.*

What are they gonna say to Reusse? Go back to Fulda?

The Reusse Rule . . . the Patrick Principles . . . they are all unofficial, of course. But they all contribute to building the profile.

Take the Best Foil Available

General managers utter the draft cliche "take the best player available." Columnists live by another: Take the best foil.

The writing gods could not possibly construct a better foil for Reusse than Sid Hartman. And Reusse played off him endlessly, tweaked him when he didn't even know he was being tweaked, roughed up Sid's sacred cows, mocked his obsession with the officiating, jousted with him in print weekly.

What a prodigious home-newspaper advantage. Most metro sports columnists need teams, players, and general managers to bounce off. Reusse certainly has identified (and eviscerated) his share. But half the time, Reusse didn't need any of them. He just needed Sid. (That the same state produced this Odd Couple of sportswriters, so utterly mismatched, and so completely dependent on one another, remains one of journalism's great miracles.)

Matter of fact, we both might have tapped that resource from time to time, and Sid might have returned the favor. Time-honored Saturday tradition: Sid entered the newsroom late morning, demanding that the copy boy print out both early Sunday columns by Reusse and Barreiro. Invariably, whatever subjects we were exploring, Sid was sure to make them part of his Sunday notes column, rebutting us before our columns had even been published.

Write Relaxed

I remember going into the doctor's office as a kid for a shot and my mother telling me: "Don't tense up when the needle goes into your arm. That's the one thing you can't do, or your arm will get really sore. Relax your arm. Breathe."

A message there for writers too.

Reusse has always struck me as the guy who not only doesn't tense up but seems to thoroughly enjoy the process that the rest of us view as root canal work. It was not all that unusual to see him wearing a grin on his face as he was clacking on the keyboard, trying out a line on himself, maybe even out loud on his newspaper colleagues. You write relaxed, you make it easier for the reader to enjoy the ride. I believe that.

Sneer at Conventional Wisdom

Whether he was taking heat over that backing-in writing style or disagreeing with just about every other writer about a coach or player or controversy, Reusse has some bleep-you to him. It has served him well. The worst columnists are like the worst sports general managers: they take the temperature of the consensus before issuing an opinion or making a judgment. The best ones don't give a damn what everybody else is writing or doing. Sometimes he has pushed back because he meant it. Sometimes he pushes back because, well, it's fun being the contrarian.

Write Like You're Still Covering a Beat

This is the one quality that drove me crazy. I am not a fast writer. Reusse is lightning. When he wrote from the road, Reusse, as a former baseball beat man, felt guilty if he did not write a column, sidebar, and notes, and then offer extra quotes to the other sidebar writer. Having rarely been a beat writer, I did not share that same guilt—until I picked up the paper the next day and I had one whole column and he produced the equivalent of 60 column inches.

Skewer Pomposity

When Reusse writes pathos and tragedy, his rule is classic "less is more." Clear, simple prose that understates everything. Let the story play out. Don't call it heartbreaking or a tragedy. Allow the details and sequence of events, often told through the principal sources, to reveal the tragedy.

Yet when it comes to skewering the insufferable, he has been quite capable of eschewing the less-is-more approach. Here, he is willing to work not only with the precision of a surgeon but with the overkill of a guillotine operator. Turkey of the Year is, more than anything else, about cutting privileged people down to size, sometimes with the subtle shot, other times with the hammer.

Work the Nicknames

The Great Man. Remarkable Mike Lynn. Everyday Eddie Guardado. Carl (Big Train) Willis. Even structures got harpooned by their association: Taj-Ma-Holtz. Taj-Ma-Zygi. Some nicknames stuck, some did not. They have become part of the sports fan's short-hand in this town.

Take Chances

Taking chances means, among other things, surprising people. When they expect you to hammer away, show some empathy. When they expect empathy, fire away.

It also means occasionally failing. And writing the wrong, politically insensitive thing. It's a dying art, in part because the pitchforks are poised these days not only to call out the swings and misses but to demand execution of the perpetrators.

Historically, what the best ones, like Reusse, have done—and were allowed to do—is get back up, dust themselves off, and jump right back in the box. Ready to swing away. Maybe even on the next pitch.

He and I used to ruminate after not quite getting the reaction we were looking for, having attempted something humorous and off the beaten opinion track. "Should have put in the satire disclaimer," we'd say to one another.

■ ■ ■

We fought rarely, disagreed occasionally. In those days in the same newsroom, Reusse was slow to boil, but could erupt. I wish I had saved the note from the time he was unhappy with the big bosses about something, probably his desire to write an extra column or two, maybe something else. Perhaps just blowing off steam. Doesn't really matter now.

He felt wronged, felt we had both been wronged. And he sent me a note to the effect that said: Bleep them. That he thought he and I consistently gave the bosses the best variety of opinion and content of any sports section in the country. And if that wasn't good enough for them, bleep 'em.

He made me feel part of something bigger that day.

Reusse has always been a valuable sounding board. I remember writing a tough Tom Kelly piece after the manager had tried to start a brawl with *Star Tribune* baseball beat writer Jeff Lenihan. The column was shorter than usual, and though I thought it said what I wanted to say, I needed to hear it from somebody else. I wanted to be sure. Reusse sat down at my chair, read it on the computer terminal, then abruptly stood up and said, "You don't need anything more. It works as it is. I'd leave it right there."

I did.

Every once in a while, long after I quit writing regularly, I'd get a text or call from him as he mulled over a risky column idea. Maybe he had already decided to write it and was just trying to reach out; maybe he was looking for that little extra nudge from somebody else. I almost always said, *Go for it.*

Like many columnists, Reusse has always liked to write about characters. Unlike most columnists, he is one. The press box changes when he walks in; there is a jolt as if everybody just sipped from the same five-hour-energy cocktail. The gravel-growl in his voice. The Frank-Gorshin-as-the-Riddler laugh. The winding yarns. The acerbic verbal volleys.

And the occasional can't-make-it-up episode.

He once kissed me on the back of my head in the Metrodome press box. It was at the end of the Vikings' historic NFC Championship Game loss to the Falcons during the 1998 playoffs. The Anderson who kicked for the Vikings missed the field goal. The Andersen who kicked for the Falcons did not.

The kiss was not so much to celebrate the loss in schadenfreude fashion as it was an acknowledgment of relief that with the loss, two columnists both known to have agitated Dennis Green from time to time would not have to absorb media blows from national reporters in the two-week lead-up to the Super Bowl.

For the record, Reusse remains the only Minnesota newspaper guy to kiss me on the head. He is also the only Minnesota newspaper guy who drove seven hours to attend my father's funeral.

INTRODUCTION

The emotions were separated by 180 degrees and yet in perfect balance as 55,155 ticketholders made their way into the Metrodome late in the afternoon of Saturday, October 26, 1991.

There was optimism, because only four years earlier the situation had been nearly identical, with the Minnesota Twins trailing their opponents (then the St. Louis Cardinals) three wins to two in the World Series. And those Twins had won the last two games in front of inspired, Homer Hanky–waving mobs to make themselves the champions of Major League Baseball. We still had the mobs in '91, equipped with a fresh supply of Homer Hankies, so why wouldn't the Twins do it again?

Weighted perfectly against that history came the pessimism of history that was less than 48 hours old: The Atlanta Braves—younger, deeper, more swashbuckling than were those Cardinals of '87—had toughed out two wins in Georgia to square the series, then sent the Twins reeling back to Minnesota after a 14–5 beatdown in Game 5.

There was also trouble in the heart of the Twins' batting order: Kirby Puckett, a legendary bad-ball hitter, was swinging at pitches even he couldn't reach.

Kent Hrbek had two hits in Game 1, famously wrestled Atlanta's Ron Gant off first base for an out in Game 2, and then went 1-for-13 at the plate in the three Atlanta losses.

Shane Mack, a sensational contributor that season, was 0-for-15 in the series and was out of the lineup for Game 5.

Plus, Scott Erickson, dealing with an ailing elbow, would be the Twins' Game 6 starter against Steve Avery, a young Atlanta lefty with a future that seemed as bright as Tom Glavine's and John Smoltz's (the latter two being eventual Hall of Famers, as it turned out).

What the fans and viewers and reporters didn't know is that the Twins had been guaranteed a victory earlier that afternoon.

That came when Puckett walked into the clubhouse and said, "Climb on my back, fellas. I got this one."

OK, Puckett might have said that 60 or 70 times a season, but this time—Game 6! Puck's Game!—he really, truly meant it. And he really, truly came through.

He tripled home Chuck Knoblauch in the bottom of the first, then scored on Mack's first hit of the series to give the Twins a 2–0 lead. He reached his glove above the plexiglass wall in left-center field to rob Ron Gant of a homer in the third. After Atlanta tied the game at 2–2 in the top of the fifth, Puckett put the Twins back ahead with a sacrifice fly in the bottom half of the inning.

The Braves tied it up again in the seventh before reliever Carl Willis struck out David Justice with his "wet sinker" to end the inning. Willis put in two more scoreless innings, and manager Tom Kelly went with closer Rick Aguilera in the 10th and again in the 11th, as the clock rolled past 11 PM.

The fans were on edge, as were the occupants of the various press boxes. No internet then, all print, and for Sunday's editions, the traditional earlier deadlines. The *Star Tribune* crew knew the presses had already started to roll for the metro edition. Thousands of newspapers were heading off to be bundled without a final score to offer among our myriad game stories, sidebars, and columns. The tributes to Puckett, already strung together but not finalized, would have a sad ring to them if this game were to be lost.

And then Atlanta manager Bobby Cox brought in Charlie Leibrandt to pitch the bottom of the 11th. Puckett was the leadoff hitter. Leibrandt was a left-hander known for his exceptional changeup. Puckett feasted on left-handers and off-speed pitches.

Later accounts revealed that Puckett's mind was racing, which was not surprising. It didn't have to be the 11th inning of Game 6 of the World Series for that to be the case with Puck. The connection between Puck's mind and mouth was a mini-version of the Indy 500—always racing fast.

During the mid-inning break, he told Chili Davis that he might bunt to get on base. Chili told him profanely to forget that, ending with something like: "Hit it out and let's go home."

Puckett then turned his attention to his South Side of Chicago pal Rick Stelmaszek, the long-serving Twins coach who was down the left-field line, running the bullpen.

Over the din of the crowd, Puckett bellowed, "Stelly! Stelly! This game is over!"

That racing mind calmed when Puckett stepped into the batter's box. He let the count get to two balls, one strike, before taking his hack.

"I had been chasing the changeups all through the series," Puckett said some time after midnight. "I was not going to do it this time. I wanted him to bring the ball up."

My description in the following day's *Star Tribune* was this: "Leibrandt delivered. The pitch was up. Puckett hitched, pumped his left leg in the manner of that baseball card hero of his, Hack Wilson, and hit a shot toward the glass in left.

"The roar started. It grew and 55,155 customers inside the Dome came to their feet. [Atlanta left fielder] Keith Mitchell ran a pass pattern out there, but it was gone, into the bleachers, into the madness."

Sportswriters had about 30 seconds to watch that madness from the press box and another five minutes to add finality to what already was on our Radio Shack TRS-80 screens, and then it was on the way to a frantic sports copy desk.

The TV viewers were blessed with hearing the grandest epitaph that could be given by a broadcaster when, as Puck's winner headed toward the seats, the great Jack Buck said: "And . . . we'll see you tomorrow night."

Almost an hour later, my all-time favorite quote from a Minnesota athlete came from the official interview room in the Metrodome. After the Game 6 prime characters, led by Puckett, had been brought in by MLB's public relations staff, the Game 7 starters—Jack Morris for the Twins and John Smoltz for the Braves—were summoned for brief interviews.

The first question asked of Morris was, "Jack, how do you feel about a chance to pitch a Game 7?"

Morris stared for a moment and then said, "Words from the late, great Marvin Gaye come to mind. 'Let's get it on.'"

"Let's get it on." Perfect.

And Marvin's words were never taken more resolutely to heart than by Morris—the notorious Black Jack: grumpiest man ever in defeat, "I got this round for everybody" in victory.

It took 10 innings for the Twins to get him a run, but it finally came when Dan Gladden hustled to second base with a broken-bat double, moved to third on a bunt, and scored on pinch-hitter Gene Larkin's fly ball over the drawn-in outfield for a 1–0 victory.

Game 7! Jack's Game!

In a long interview that took place during the pandemic shutdown in 2020, Gladden, the scorer of the championship-clinching run in Game 7, remembered this about the end to Game 6: "We celebrated on the field after Puck's home run, and we were still running around in the clubhouse, screaming.

"And then a few of us saw Morris. He walked in, put his glove down, took off his hat, and stared into the locker—all business already for Game 7.

"I remember saying, 'Look at this guy. He's not going to get beat.'"

The first pitch of Game 6 was thrown by Scott Erickson at 7:28 PM on October 26, 1991. Gladden stepped on home plate at 11:01 PM on October 27.

Those 27½ hours of high anxiety—whether it was based on "how much more Hanky waving can my arm take?" or the sound of running presses dancing in your head—remain the greatest drama, the greatest competition we've had in our midst in my period of full sports consciousness, which I've decided dates to age eight in 1954.

Yet, to make sure we didn't get too confident in our standing as the envy of America, four days later, on Halloween, it started to snow, and before it stopped, the Twin Cities had received 31 inches.

Ecstasy, followed by days of pushing strangers' cars out of snowdrifts. That's us.

Games 6 and 7 of the 1991 World Series were epic for all of us; yet, for me, they are no more fondly remembered than the stories and characters that can be found during a thousand drives to the corners of Minnesota.

The following tale is an example of what can be found at the end of one of those drives—a small-town story so terrific that you can't wait to get to your keyboard and start writing, and unexpected gems that remind why you love being a sportswriter.

It was my second month since moving to the *Star Tribune* in July 1988, and I had arranged to interview Heather Van Norman at her family's home in Windom. Heather had completed her high school athletic career in June by winning the 100-meter, 200-meter, and 400-meter races in the Class A state meet. It was her fourth straight season doing so, making this the "quadruple triple" in Windom Eagles athletic lore.

The result was two of the most entertaining hours of my reporting career, simply because every moment was real family dynamics. Millie and Don Van Norman had three children: daughter Pat and sons Larry and Alan. Larry had died at age 12 in the winter of 1965 when he was playing with a friend in a nearby gravel pit. A huge ice formation fell on him.

Thirteen years after youngest son Alan was born, the Van

Normans decided they wanted another little girl. They adopted two biracial infants, Mark and Heather, from a Minneapolis adoption agency.

The youngsters were raised in lily-white Windom. Heather said of her hometown: "I've never been made to feel different here—never."

That summer of 1988 she was feeling different, however: anxious to get on with her life, and bored because her friends were either working or on family trips.

"Is it hard to get a summer job in Windom?" I asked Heather.

Father Don, who was home on his lunch break from the post office, beat his daughter to an answer: "It depends on if you look or not."

Millie and Heather laughed. The secret was out: Heather Van Norman's energy shown in winning her final 147 races in high school did not carry over to household chores or a summer job.

"A lot of kids in town pick on me about it," Heather said. "The other day, I told a couple of guys I had to go home and vacuum. They said, 'Oh, my god,' and pretended like they were going to pass out from the shock."

Heather would spend one year running track for the University of Minnesota Gophers, then transferred to Louisiana State University. She had an excellent career there, although it was interrupted for a year when she became pregnant. The father of the child was Odell Beckham, an LSU football player. She graduated from LSU in 1995 having been named a six-time All-American. Heather later married Olympic sprinter Derek Mills while raising her son, Odell Beckham Jr.

I've talked with her a couple of times about that interesting lad of hers, who would go on to have a memorable career in the NFL. Heather's comment on Odell Jr.'s talent: "He hit the genetic jackpot."

On that day in 1988, I already had cost Heather her daily viewings of *The Young and the Restless* and *Days of Our Lives*, and I headed back to the Twin Cities with a full notebook and driving a familiar route.

Windom is 24 miles from my hometown of Fulda. We took this trip seven, eight times a year as a family in the 1950s, often with a Minneapolis Millers baseball game, or a pro rasslin' card, or—the real prize—a state basketball tournament at Williams Arena as the reward at the end of the journey.

I was impatient to reach the Twin Cities during those childhood trips, and I was impatient to get there in July 1988. I had collected some good stuff in my conversation with the Van Normans, and I was excited to get home and start hackin'.

1

THE PRIDE OF FULDA

Any attempt to trace Patrick Reusse's Hall of Fame journalism career must begin at its root, in the tiny southern Minnesota town of Fulda. And just like his career, his upbringing followed a unique path filled with colorful stories and characters. He lived above a funeral home, the son of an undertaker who also ran the town baseball team, was involved in the annual smoked carp festival, and pulled more than his fair share of hijinks.

■ ■ ■

I was born October 17, 1945—somewhere. I started out in an orphanage. I was 10 months old before I got adopted. I was a fat little kid, and the people who came in looking to adopt must not have been impressed. The prospective mothers probably didn't want to get a bad back carrying this fat baby around.

My birth name was James Patrick Malley, and I'm a full-blooded Irishman.

After 10 months in the orphanage, I was adopted by Richard and Cecile Reusse of Fulda, Minnesota. They had adopted another son—my brother, Michael—five years earlier; then they adopted a daughter—my sister, Meg—three years after they adopted me.

My dad was 40 years and two days older than me. His name was Richard, but most everybody in Fulda knew him as Dick. My

< 9 >

mom came from an Irish clan. My dad was very close to my mom's family. He fit perfectly with the goofy Irishmen.

My brother had many more memories of our father's hijinks with baseball and other stuff. A lot of my stories about Richard I learned from my brother.

My father was the town undertaker in Fulda, which is about three hours southwest of the Twin Cities. When I was a young kid, the funeral home was in downtown Fulda, and we lived in an apartment nearby. Later my family built a place out on the lake, and it was my mom's dream home. I look at it now and it seems very small, but at the time I thought, *Wow.*

We eventually sold that house, and my dad transformed an apartment building he owned next door into a living area for us upstairs and the funeral home downstairs, complete with embalming room. Most of my childhood memories are from living there. It was great. We had windows looking out over the lake all the way around the front of the house.

Living above a funeral home felt normal to me. It was always fun to frighten the hell out of my buddies when we had a body in the back room. I'd say, "Come on, we'll take the shortcut to the back." We'd go in and there'd be a body to be prepared and my friends would take off running.

My dad had three brothers and three sisters. They owned a furniture store called Reusse Bros. on Main Street that went back to the late 1800s. As with many towns in rural America back then, the furniture store guy was also the town undertaker. My father was the youngest son, and he was the only member of the family to go to mortuary science school. He went to the U, and that's where he met my mom. He developed some great friends while at mortuary science school. The undertaker conventions were legendary; they would gather in the Twin Cities and get hammered.

I always said that being an undertaker was good for my father. A typical year would be 40 funerals. For each funeral, he'd pick up the body and embalm it—that's one day. The next day is the wake, and the burial is the day after. That's three days per funeral.

Multiply by 40, and that's 120 days of working, which means my dad had 245 days to hunt, fish, worry about baseball, and think up other schemes.

My father loved baseball. He helped run the local townball team, the Fulda Giants, and was the manager from 1948 to 1950. Townball was a huge deal back in the late 1940s and through the early '60s. My dad was a big baseball promoter.

During this era of townball, players were paid by the teams, and all the towns would recruit and pay their players. Richard would hit up the farmers and businessmen around Fulda to raise money so that the Giants could sign guys. He would get his good buddy Don Schwab to write out a check to the Fulda Baseball Association for $500. Then he'd go all over town and say, "You're not going to let that cheap Schwab give more money than you are, are you?" He'd go to the bankers, the businesses, and the farmers, holding that check. He'd say, "Look at this, even that cheap Schwab gave me five hundred dollars."

After he was done, he'd go back to Schwab and rip up his check and have him write one for $200. They'd run the "Cheap Schwab" scam every year. Don was a good guy. He always called my dad "Dickie."

I remember my mom complaining about how much money Richard kicked away on baseball. I'm sure he was spending two or three grand a year of his own money.

Around this time, the big push was to get lights installed at the townball parks. There was a league in southern Minnesota called the First Night League. It was going to be one of the first leagues in which every team had lights so they could play night games.

In 1949 the baseball boosters wanted the city—basically the taxpayers—to pay for lights so that Fulda could be part of the First Night League. A referendum was to be held in September for the townspeople to vote on whether to pay for the lights. The team knew it had to do something dramatic to sway the voters. That's when Richard signed two Black ballplayers in the hope of attracting people to the ballpark.

One was Hilton Smith, a pitcher who was later inducted into the National Baseball Hall of Fame. He was Satchel Paige's running mate with the Kansas City Monarchs of the Negro American League. By this time, Smith's arm was wrecked, and the Monarchs let him go. My dad went to Kansas City, found him, and signed him. The Smith family lived in a back apartment in the building my dad owned (before he had converted it into the funeral home and Reusse family residence). Hilton's son played little league baseball in Fulda.

The other guy my dad brought in to play for the Fulda Giants was Earl Ashby, who was a catcher and pitcher from Cuba. Ashby probably made as much money playing in Fulda as he could have been making in professional baseball.

Many years later, I met the Smith family because Hilton went into the Hall of Fame the same year as Kirby Puckett, in 2001, and his family was in Cooperstown for the induction ceremony. Hilton had passed away in 1983.

After he retired, Hilton lived in Kansas City, and one time in the early 1980s when I was there covering a Twins series I said to myself, *Why have I never gone to see Hilton?* I looked in the phone book and found his number. We had a nice conversation. Great guy. I told him, "Next time I'm in town, let's have lunch." He died that winter, so I never got to meet him in person.

The Smith and Ashby signings helped bring in big crowds for the Fulda Giants, and the team got into the First Night League in 1950 after the town referendum passed. The league had teams from Marshall, Worthington, and some of the bigger towns. Iona, which is a tiny little town between Fulda and Slayton, was a major rival.

Slayton and Fulda were also rivals, and we would always try to torment the Slayton players and fans. The towns were 12 miles apart. Both towns had high schools, but Slayton was bigger than us. The schools played each other in basketball for the "Goat," which was a homemade trophy. It was the ugliest trophy ever.

Slayton's baseball team was the Rockets. One time, my dad had guys set up rockets to shoot off along the road between Fulda and Slayton. After Fulda won the game and Slayton fans started heading home, almost like a caravan, one of my old man's helpers shot up a big rocket about a mile outside of town. As the fans continued on to Slayton, the rockets kept getting smaller and smaller. By the end, it was a little buzz bomb. Dad just loved to torment Slayton.

In addition to his townball responsibilities, Richard also coached the Little League team for a few years. He thought they were a bit shy in talent, so he recruited two short 15-year-olds: Bernie Beckman and my cousin Eddie. The only problem was they both needed to shave by then—they were three years past the league's age limit. Slayton's Little League tournament was held in conjunction with the Murray County fair. Worried that the rival teams might be suspicious of him, Richard was a no-show to the tournament. He had my mother and a neighbor named Mabel coach the team, knowing there would not be as many insults about cheating hurled at them. The team claimed the first-place trophy.

After taking a break from townball for a few years, my dad got back into it, and in '56 the Fulda Giants jumped into the Western Minny, which was the powerhouse league and included teams from Springfield, Marshall, and New Ulm.

One time, my father ran an ad in the local paper saying that the Fulda ballpark was mosquito-free for Giants games. That was a common complaint—"I'm not going to the game. Too many mosquitoes"—so all the kids in town were out catching mosquitoes. Twenty-five bucks for a live mosquito, the ad claimed. The kids would hand a mosquito to Richard. He'd squish it and say, "That's not a live mosquito."

In 1956 one of the players he signed was Jack McCartan, who was a slugger for the Gophers team that won the NCAA title that June. McCartan went on to be the goalie on the 1960 Olympic hockey team. Richard also hired Don Brummer, who was a very good shortstop from Creighton. He then built a Little League ballpark behind our house and paid McCartan and Brummer to coach me and my buddies. My dad lost a lot of money that year, or at least I remember my mom complaining about it.

Another top player for Fulda around this time was Jerry Thomas, who pitched for Fulda in 1955. Thomas would be named the College World Series MVP with the Gophers championship team in 1956, and he later was inducted into the university's sports hall of fame. He was the ace for the Fulda squad, but nobody was coming to games. My father decided they needed to do what they had done in '49: sign Black players. So Richard headed to Kansas City with his right-hand man, Sid Covert.

Sid and Richard didn't know where they were going to find players. The legend is that they stopped at a bar down there and heard two guys bragging about all the home runs they hit. Sid and Richard signed the two guys then and there, promising them money and opportunity.

One guy was named Duffy and the other was Jameson, and the four of them drove back to Fulda in our family station wagon. They got to about the Iowa border when Richard and Sid realized the guys were bragging about softball, not baseball. But they had already taken the plunge.

Richard went driving around Fulda and other small towns, announcing on a speaker mounted to the top of the family station wagon: "Come and see the two great Negro ballplayers: Triple Duty Duffy and Cannonball Jameson."

Fulda played a doubleheader that Sunday against Wilmont, which had signed Jerry Thomas. The Giants got beat 15–0 and 15–1. These two guys couldn't play baseball. Richard took them to Worthington and put them on a bus back to Kansas City.

I went to Brown's bar in Fulda with my dad the next day. He received more abuse than Ron Davis did as a closer for the Twins.

My older brother, Michael, and I were both sports nuts from being around my dad. My first memories of being a fan are from 1954, when I was eight years old. I don't think we had a TV at that point, but I have vivid memories of the '54 World Series. I considered myself quite the sports aficionado because I regularly in-spected the newspaper sports section. I always said that I learned to count by 7s instead of 10s because of touchdowns. If you see the number 13, it's because someone missed an extra point.

I lost 50 cents to my uncle Harry because of the 1954 World Series. The Cleveland Indians had popped up and beat the New York Yankees to claim the American League pennant by winning 111 games. They were playing Willie Mays and the New York Giants in the World Series. Uncle Harry was a National League fan, and he bet me 50 cents that the Giants would win. I thought I had fooled him. How can Cleveland not win? They went 111–43 that season.

The Giants swept Cleveland in four games. The first game of the series featured Willie Mays's amazing catch at the Polo Grounds in New York. I know the photos, but we didn't see it on TV. I'll never forget handing my uncle Harry those two quarters, which I borrowed from my father. I was ashamed of my lack of baseball knowledge.

In addition to baseball, my dad loved pro wrestling. He loved going to matches and agitating the crowds. He always rooted for the villains. He'd get the whole crowd riled up. One time when I was a kid, Richard and my uncle Frank, one of my mom's brothers, took me to a wrestling match in St. Paul. We went to see Verne Gagne wrestling some villain, and my dad was yelling, "Verne's cheating! He's cheating!" The rest of the crowd went nuts, all stirred up. Wrestling fans took it seriously. They all wanted to fight my dad.

■ ■ ■

When my dad wasn't at a ball field, hunting and fishing were his big things. Hunting was a large part of our life. He was known to exceed the limits on pheasants and ducks and also would some-how manage to get a netting license for the Des Moines River, which wound around in that area. Allegedly, the game fish caught in the net would be used to stock Fulda Lake, but the most edible walleye somehow had a tendency to end up in our freezer.

Richard had recruited brother Michael and his best pal, Dickie Overlees, to help with the net through a stretch of the river. They would make a swath, pull the net into shore, and pull out the game fish. One day I was walking along the shore with my mom observing this, and they found a big snapping turtle in the net. Overlees grabbed it by the tail and tossed it in front of me, and that was the first time my mother ever heard me use an f-bomb.

Overlees was an outstanding basketball player on one of Fulda's best teams ever, in 1958–59. He also was a premier agitator. He was the one who gave me my Fulda nickname "Grease" because of the large amount of Brylcreem I applied to my hair as a grade-schooler.

Pheasants were like chickens in southwest Minnesota in the 1950s. Ezra Taft Benson was President Eisenhower's secretary of agriculture, and he came up with the Soil Bank Program, which means paying farmers not to grow crops. Just let the fields go wild. Ezra Taft later became the head of the Mormon Church. He was a hero to us because the Soil Bank Program meant there was so much wild land and there were pheasants everywhere. You could go out after school and drive around and shoot four pheasants every day.

We also had the duck-hunting slough at Badger Lake, so we'd hunt ducks in the morning and pheasants in the afternoon. During my freshman year, I broke my arm and had to sit out from football. I was so happy because I could still put the .410 shotgun across my cast and shoot pheasants out the car window and I didn't have to play football.

About 15 miles away was a game reserve called Talcot Lake, and when it started to get cold in November, thousands of mallards would sit there. The ducks would leave the lake in the morning, and a flock of about 150 would go into a cornfield and feast. They'd have to stop and get a drink of water on the way back to Talcot. That first day when there was a cold, strong, northwest wind, it would be a bonanza for those of us lucky enough to be in our blind in "Kill 'em Bay." The ducks would come in to get a drink, and you'd shoot the hell out of them.

My uncle Carl was the best marksman I've ever seen in my life, even though he was in his 70s when I was hunting with him. As a kid I liked to shoot any single duck I possibly could. But Uncle Carl would say, "Wait, wait, wait." When you hunted with him, he would wait for two mallards to cross in the air and then get both of them with one shot. He was a two-for-one guy.

My dad loved to deer hunt too. He'd go up to the north woods and bring them home. Which reminds me of an all-time classic Richard story. One winter, he was driving back from hunting and he'd got a buck deer. Nice set of antlers.

Christmas wasn't that far away, and he decided to drop by and have a little fun with his buddy from mortuary science school, Kenny Malone, who had a bunch of little kids. My dad stopped somewhere on the way to Kenny's and got some Christmas bells, a harness, and some red nail polish. He painted a red nose on the deer and attached the bells to the harness.

He pulled into the Malones' driveway. Somehow he got the kids to come outside first, and he apologized to them for ruining Christmas because he shot Rudolph. Kenny's wife went nuts. Man, he was quite the agitator.

My mother's family, the McDonoughs of Waldorf, Minnesota, had some real characters too. Uncle Art was the golden child of the family because he was a vice president at Mars candy company in New Jersey. Art would come back to Minnesota maybe once every three years, and when he did it was a big deal. Art was a goofball.

My mother's family all assembled in Portland, Oregon, one summer for my cousin Judy's wedding. Richard took Art on an excursion the day before the wedding. We were having a big family dinner at Aunt Grace's home that afternoon, and Richard and Art were late coming back for it. When they finally got there, Art tripped over the front door stoop and fell down face first, sliding in on his belly. Everybody was screaming at my old man for getting Art drunk.

My mom was great. A beautiful Irish woman. She loved to sing, and the cats in the neighborhood would screech when she did. She had this god-awful voice, but she thought she could sing, especially when she got some whiskey in her.

Because he was in the funeral business, my dad knew all the priests and ministers from the area. We went to every church dinner there was. We gave away Lutheran calendars and Catholic calendars. On the Tuesday before Ash Wednesday the priests would come to our house and drink because they were all giving up alcohol for Lent. On one such occasion, they were in the kitchen with my mother singing "Danny Boy." It was midnight, and Richard came out of the bedroom and said, "All right, go to bed. You guys go home."

The big social event in Fulda for years was the smoked carp feed. Fish-O-Rama, they called it. Naturally, Richard was in on it. There was a guy in town named Flat. Nobody knows what Flat did, but he was the expert fish smoker. And he was also the expert at making graupenwurst—a sausage made with pork, barley, a little bit of blood, and great spices. It was fantastic.

The Fulda Game and Fish Club would seine the lakes in the middle of January and get hundreds of pounds of carp. They'd open a hole in the ice, and the carp would come up to breathe in the air. They'd butcher like 2,000 pounds of carp. They would get drunk for three days and be butchering carp, and then they would smoke it. Eating smoked carp is great, but the odor sticks with you. They'd have a big dance on a Saturday night. How is that for a pickup line: "Hey, you want to go to the smoked carp dance?"

It was unbelievable.

My mom died in 1962. Breast cancer. She was diagnosed in '59. I was in high school then, and nobody would give the kids any information. All the adults in the family knew she was dying, but I didn't. She had been at the Mayo Clinic, where they pulled out all the stops to find a cure. Then she was moved to the Slayton hospital to be closer to home. I drove to the hospital one night. I hadn't seen her in a few days. That evening it hit me that this was it. She died the next day.

Richard had already made plans to sell the funeral home. Mom died in May, and we moved by the middle of June. He wanted to be near the Twin Cities and go to ball games. We moved to Prior Lake for my senior year of high school.

2

◆

FINDING A CALLING IN NORTHERN MINNESOTA

Before he became a big-city sportswriter, Reusse cut his teeth in journalism in Duluth and then St. Cloud. He was a novice at writing a story initially, and he made a pittance in salary, but his love of those places still runs deep more than 50 years later.

■ ■ ■

I started going to the University of Minnesota in the fall of 1963. Then I got married and had a child. I was also working at United Van Bus near the north side, just off Glenwood Avenue. This job lasted about four months. I was writing down the prices for delivering stuff. It was brutally boring.

There were nice people who worked there. A guy named Dale came in as an accountant, and we became buddies because he was also a drinker. One weekend Dale, my brother, and I drove up to Bemidji for Vikings training camp. I didn't have that much interest in Vikings training camp, but I went for the laughs. We got hammered for a couple of days and then drove back. Dale picked up the bar tabs; we figured he was just a good guy.

Turns out Dale was embezzling from the company.

When the company told me about Dale, they wondered if I was

< 21 >

in on it and how much I knew about Dale being a crook. I said, "You know what, we've come to the end of the road here."

Luckily, I was also working as a copy boy at the *Minneapolis Morning Tribune*. When the other job went south, I went to the newspaper and talked them into letting me work more hours. I started working there five days a week, and I loved it. I was 20 years old at the time.

I got hired at the Minneapolis paper in August 1963, when I was 17. I had just gotten out of high school at Prior Lake. My father knew Ted Peterson, who was the outstate sports editor. Ted mostly covered prep sports, but he also covered amateur baseball. My dad knew him from running the Fulda Giants.

My father called up Ted and said, "You need somebody down there to answer phones. I know the person for you."

That's how I got the job. I was doing entry-level stuff: answering phones, running errands, fetching photos from the newsroom library.

I worked just Friday through Sunday in '63. I would take calls about high school sports on Friday nights. Saturdays were chaotic because you had a lot of events taking place locally and the Sunday sports section was the largest of the week. On Sundays, the Vikings played, but it was more laid back usually.

From the first day I was in there, I loved the vibe and the activity of the newsroom, everybody giving each other a hard time and barking at each other and then going out drinking together.

Bob Sorensen ran the *Tribune*'s night desk at the time. He later became the books editor. "Sorehead," as we called him, was the hero of my youth. I loved that guy. He'd bring me to the bar with the other guys, even when I was a 17-year-old copy boy. I thought to myself, *This is great. I'm at the bar with all these guys, and they're buying the 20-cent beers.*

By then, I knew the newspaper world was where I wanted to be. But I couldn't be a copy boy my whole life. Somebody told me the *Duluth News Tribune* had an opening and to go see Bruce Bennett, the sports editor up there.

I lined up an interview and drove to Duluth. Nobody warned me that Bruce's arms ended at his elbows, a deformity from birth. I walked in, and he stuck out his arm for a handshake. I didn't know what to do. We got off to a rough start, but he was an amazing guy.

The pay was $76.08 a week. I think they would have hired a wino off the street, but Bruce hired me instead. My first day was December 27, 1965.

We had some legends up there. Davis Helberg was a great writer. Dick Gerzic was the guy Bruce told to teach me how to write a story and work the desk. I had never written or edited a story. I had typed up two graphs for local golf tournaments. That was it. I was a complete novice.

One of the first nights I was there, Esko called in its high school basketball box score. All Finlanders. As a boy from Fulda who had never met a Finlander, I had no chance of getting those names right.

Another twist that winter was that we had to cover the regional bonspiels, or curling competitions, that took place on weekends. Our curling reporter was a guy name Knobby Clark. He was also the skipper on one of the best teams in the area. So on several occasions I took dictation from Knobby Clark as he quoted the winner, Knobby Clark.

After a couple of weeks, I started getting more writing assignments, although we didn't get bylines at first. The editors put me on the Duluth Hornets senior hockey team, which played at the Curling Club on Sundays. That was the first hockey I ever witnessed in person. Connie Pleban, a US Hockey Hall of Famer, ran the Hornets. I went to him and said, "Connie, I don't know what the hell is going on here. Can you help me?" Connie and a couple other guys taught me the basics.

I also started writing advances for high school basketball games and then covering the games. This was 1966, when Duluth East went to the state championship game against Edina in one-class basketball. East's coach was Joe Mrkonich, and we became quick buddies.

Sid Peterson was the slot guy at the *News Tribune*; he was the editor responsible for laying out the articles. He was a veteran newspaper guy in his 70s and had been a hard drinker in his day. No matter what you wrote for that Friday's upcoming high school basketball games, it would be a two-column, 36-point headline that read, "Hot Cage Duels on Tap Tonight." You could have Duluth East and Central playing in the battle of the century, or two bad teams playing in a nothing game, no matter what the lede to your story was, the headline was always "Hot Cage Duels on Tap Tonight."

The big Duluth Entertainment Convention Center was built in 1966, and it became the new hockey arena in the city. It was also the University of Minnesota Duluth's first year in the Western Collegiate Hockey Association; they had been playing an independent Division I schedule for a few years. UMD was also playing its final season in the old Curling Club.

There are so many memories from my time in Duluth that it seems like I was there for five years, but it was only four months.

Meanwhile, Jon Roe of the *St. Cloud Times* had decided to go back to college—again—and the paper needed someone to take his place. Jon had been at the *Times* for eight years. He'd go to school, drop out, work for the *Times*, then go back to school and work part-time for the *Times*.

Fortunately, I had become buddies with Mike Augustin when I worked as a copy boy in Minneapolis, and Augie was now the sports editor in St. Cloud. Earlier, Augie had come to the Twin Cities from the *St. Cloud Times* to finish his degree at the U. He went for a couple of semesters and worked as a copy boy with us before returning to St. Cloud.

When I found out the *Times* had an opening, I called Augie from Duluth and said, "Get me out of here." I went down for an interview and met the managing editor, Chuck Rathe. Then Augie and I went to a bar. That was the interview. The pay was $110 a week, but I had to work 52 hours. I thought I had died and gone to heaven. I left Duluth on May 2 in a driving snowstorm.

I was in St. Cloud for two and a half years. The most fun in my life, man. We had Augie, and Jon Roe was a part-timer, along with the great Frankie Hyland, who was also going back to college part-time. He was from Little Falls and was just a character. We were all buds, and we all liked our beer.

Frankie later went to West Palm Beach and then ended up in Atlanta working for the *Atlanta Journal* for many years. Atlanta Hawks star Pete Maravich once threatened to shoot him in a *Sport* magazine story. Another time, Frankie was at dinner with Falcons coach Norm Van Brocklin before a game. Van Brocklin was tuned up. He started making fun of Frankie's long hair. Frankie responded by calling Van Brocklin a "loser." Van Brocklin got ahold of Frankie's tie and was trying to choke him. Frankie was gasping but still managed to get out one more "You're a loser." Then, later on, Frankie did something to make Hank Aaron mad. Aaron smashed a bowl of strawberries in his face over something he had written. I told Frankie he had an Atlanta hat trick, pissing off Pete Maravich, Norm Van Brocklin, and Hank Aaron.

Back at the *Times* in '66, '67, Augie covered St. John's University and St. Cloud Tech, and I covered Cathedral High School and St. Cloud State. With Jon and Frankie's help, we covered the whole Stearns County area. We had a hell of a staff.

We also had some incredible coaches in town, including John Gagliardi, the St. John's football coach, and Red Severson, the St. Cloud State basketball coach. Jim Smith was still relatively new as the basketball coach at St. John's, and he had some good teams right off the bat. Plus Cathedral High and St. Cloud Tech were both great athletically. But Johnnies football and Huskies basketball were definitely the number one and two things in St. Cloud when I was there.

One time I was doing a recruiting story with Red. He was going to Willmar to see a high school game, and I told Red I wanted to do a piece on how he scouted players, really get in-depth.

Red took a $50 advance from the university to make the trip. We started at the Ace Bar across the bridge in east St. Cloud. Red bought steaks, and then we went to Beaudreau's Bar. Red was in there arm wrestling with guys until midnight. The recruiting trip to Willmar wound up being about 15 blocks from the campus. Around one o'clock in the morning, I realized the recruiting story I promised Augie for prominent display two days from now might need some remodeling. I can't remember what I ended up writing, but it certainly wasn't the story I pitched.

Red's St. Cloud teams were great. Terry Porter and Tom Ditty were the Huskies' top stars in those days. I was the same age as the players, and we would have beers together. That was objective writing, right? *Hey, hell of a game, guys. I've got to write my story. I'll see you at the Press Bar later.*

Porter had been a star on the '63 Marshall High team that beat Cloquet in probably the greatest state championship game ever. He could shoot it with the best of them. Slower than hell, though. He was called "Turk" because he stuck out his butt when he was running. He looked like a turkey.

Red started the Granite City Classic college basketball tournament. It was big-time by St. Cloud standards. Great teams would come to play. We covered that thing like it was the Final Four.

Every night after the games, the Legion Club basement was the place to be. All the coaches would be there. Forddy Anderson, who had been the coach at Michigan State, brought in a team from a short-lived college in Nebraska called Hiram Scott. That outfit had some good athletes, if not exactly scholars.

In 1967 the National Association of Intercollegiate Athletics all-stars worked out in St. Cloud for four or five days before they played in the Pan Am Games qualifying tournament at Williams Arena in Minneapolis. They played an exhibition game against the Huskies about six weeks after St. Cloud's season ended. The arena was packed that night. Future NBA players including Al "Where's the Fire?" Tucker of Oklahoma Baptist and Earl "The Pearl" Monroe of Winston-Salem State played for the NAIA all-stars. Basketball was *huge* in the St. Cloud area.

I was introduced to the intense St. Thomas–St. John's rivalry around this time too. St. John's played basketball in Guild Hall, affectionately known as "Rat Hall" back then. It held about 800 people. St. Thomas played at O'Shaughnessy Hall, which everyone called the "Hot Box." That gym was on the third floor of an ancient athletic facility.

The Tommies coach was Tom Feely, who was about five-foot-four and very short-tempered. His son, Pat Feely, was the point guard. Poor Pat. Whenever he'd get the ball, the whole Johnnies crowd would chant, "Daddy! Daddy! Daddy!" He'd give up the ball, and the crowd would go silent. Then he'd get it back, and it was "Daddy! Daddy! Daddy!" It didn't seem to bother Pat, but the old man's head would turn absolutely red.

St. Thomas also had some stellar big men under Feely. Steve Fritz, who stood about six-foot-five, was a great inside player. After graduating in 1971, he became an assistant coach under Feely and then was the head coach for 31 years as well as the school's athletic director from 1992 to 2018. The seven-foot-three Bob Rosier graduated in 1974 and was selected by the Chicago Bulls in the sixth round of that year's NBA draft, although he never played in the league.

The Johnnies–Tommies games were always great. One night, Augie and I went down to St. Thomas for a game in the Hot Box. It was Senior Night, and the school was honoring another Minnesota Intercollegiate Athletic Conference championship team. They turned off the lights in the arena for the introductions and shined a spotlight on a big hoop covered with crepe paper. The Tommies were going to run triumphantly through the hoop onto the court. Just as you could hear the *clomp, clomp, clomp* of the players running across the court, a St. John's student ran through the hoop. The Tommie fans started beating the crap out of this kid in the middle of the court. It was unbelievable.

St. John's–St. Thomas was definitely my favorite Minnesota rivalry. Now that St. Thomas has moved to Division I, there's a void in the MIAC that will never be replaced. And for certain there is nobody on this planet I miss more than Mike Augustin, who died in 1997 after a short bout with pancreatic cancer.

Augie was man about many different central Minnesota towns during his St. Cloud days. For example, in 1961 the state high school league kicked Minneapolis Roosevelt out of the state basketball tournament the day before it started because of some absurd player ineligibility. As a replacement, they chose Royalton, which had lost to Roosevelt in the Region 5 semifinals. Tournament officials tracked down Royalton coach Wally Chute at a bar after midnight to inform him that he needed to get his team to the Twin Cities. Augie's determined reporting allowed him to get an immediate reaction from Chute for the next day's *St. Cloud Times*. It helped that he was sitting next to Chute at the bar.

I was in St. Cloud from May of '66 until September of '68. I still have great affinity for St. Cloud, and I met some truly amazing and colorful characters.

The St. Cloud Rox of the Northern League were the Minnesota Twins' minor league affiliate at the time. Kenny Staples was the manager. He was a beauty. He wanted to win every freaking game.

Augie and I would have breakfast with Kenny at nine o'clock many mornings. He would get these calls on the pay phone, and he and George Brophy, who was the Twins' farm director, would be arguing with each other. Kenny never got the concept of player development. He just wanted to win.

At Rox games, the beer vendor was Albie Peckskamp. When we wanted some beers upstairs in the press box, we'd announce over the PA system, "Would 1–1–4 please report to the press box." And Albie would look up and say, "Four?" That kind of gave away the secret 1–1 code.

So many great memories. I sure loved it up there.

3

◆

THE START OF A BIG-CITY CAREER

Reusse's five-plus decades of sportswriting in the Twin Cities includes lengthy stints on both sides of the Mississippi River. He started by covering high school sports and eventually became a columnist. His favorite period came when he was assigned to the Twins beat in 1974. He loved being a "ball writer"—back then and still to this day.

■ ■ ■

I came to St. Paul in September 1968, about a month shy of my twenty-third birthday. I had been working at the *St. Cloud Times*, where I had replaced Jon Roe as a full-timer. Jon had gotten hired by the *Minneapolis Morning Tribune* in 1967, where he was helping to cover golf.

Over in St. Paul, Ken Murphy was the golf writer for the *Pioneer Press* and the afternoon *Dispatch*, as well as the morning sports editor. There was only one sports staff, so writers wrote for both papers. They would cover a game for the morning edition and then do a second story for the afternoon paper.

As the morning sports editor, Murph basically did all the grunt work. In the summer of 1968 Murph was looking for sportswriters because a bunch of guys had left the paper. Roe saw Murph at a golf tournament, where he was lamenting that the *Pioneer Press*

< 29 >

needed help. Roe told him, "Well, get the guy up in St. Cloud. Get Reusse." I came down in late August for an interview, and they hired me. My first night on the desk was Labor Day of 1968.

I spent two years as the main prep writer. It was helpful that I had been in Duluth and had actually seen a couple of hockey games while I was there. Now that I was the prep editor, I was doing the state high school hockey rankings as well as state basketball rankings for the *Pioneer Press*. I was a bit overmatched in the area of puck expertise.

The next two winters—1968–69 and '69–70—I basically spent every Saturday at Aldrich Arena on the east side of St. Paul. There was always a tripleheader. Aldrich Arena is where the schools from the northern suburbs played their games, and some of the city conference games were played there. The Catholic schools played there too.

The year 1969 was a turning point in high school sports. It was the beginning of the era when the state hockey tournament became a huge event—so big that Howard Cosell came in to cover it—and it eventually surpassed the basketball tournament for popularity and media attention, which was incomprehensible to those of us who grew up in the '50s and '60s. By the '70s high school hockey was becoming big all over the state, beyond the Twin Cities, Duluth and the Iron Range, and the northwest corner of the state, which had long been hockey hotbeds.

In 1969 the hockey tournament moved out of the old St. Paul Auditorium and to the Met Center in Bloomington, which had opened two years earlier with the arrival of the Minnesota North Stars. Now all of a sudden the hockey tournament could draw 15,000 fans instead of the 9,000 that could be accommodated in the old auditorium.

That year, when the tournament still had just one class, tiny Warroad took on suburban Edina in the championship game. The Edina Hornets had never won a state title at that point, but they were already the hated cake-eaters as a large suburban power. That year, the public got a good look at big versus small in hockey.

Warroad skated three defensemen and two lines. Edina was skating four defensemen and three lines, which was a big deal back then because it showed their roster depth and size. Edina had their spiffy green-and-white uniforms, and Coach Willard Ikola always wore his trademark houndstooth hat.

I had seen Warroad play that winter at Drake Arena at St. Paul Academy. I had heard about Henry Boucha, this Native American kid from Warroad. Even as a hockey novice, I could tell he was something special as soon as I saw him play that night. He would get the puck and . . . look out. He started getting publicity in the Twin Cities. It was his senior year. We built him up as best we could heading into the state tournament.

Warroad got to the championship game after defeating their longtime rival Roseau in the semis. Edina trounced South St. Paul, the previous year's championship runner-up.

During the championship game, a kid on Edina named Jim Knutson, who was a nice guy, hit Boucha hard into the boards and knocked him down. Henry had to leave the game. It was bad.

Other than the 2,500 Edina people who had tickets, the crowd in the arena couldn't have been more hostile to the Hornets.

Edina was ahead 3–2 when Boucha went out and then took a 4–2 lead, but Warroad rallied back and tied it up at four, sending the game into overtime. Edina ended up winning the game and claimed their first title of many to come. As the players celebrated on the ice, fans were screaming, booing the living hell out of Edina. It was unbelievable. It really brought attention and emotion to what was the tournament's biggest-ever audience.

The basketball tournament was still a big deal too. The 1970 tournament was the last year of a one-class tournament, and within five or six years the division into multiple classes really detracted from the event.

Not in 1970, though, when Sherburn, a little town in southern Minnesota, beat South St. Paul for the championship. The crowd was rooting heavily for Sherburn, which had two great players in Jeff McCarron and Tom Mulso.

The hockey tournament was played a month before basketball back then because the Minnesota State High School League wanted to have packed gyms for a full month of basketball, with two weeks of districts, one week of regionals, and then one week of the state tournament.

The *Minneapolis Tribune* would print the eight-team basketball bracket in the paper all week. Everybody threw in two bucks to pick the bracket, including my mother's bridge club.

The *Tribune* would send out reporters to all eight towns that had teams in the tournament to do stories. It was a huge late-March happening.

■ ■ ■

That was the backdrop to my start in St. Paul. When I started, the newspapers were notorious for not paying well, even though we had a guild. People wonder why I'm an old union guy. In two years I went from earning 145 bucks a week in salary to $325 a week because of increased seniority and a new guild contract. They weren't paying me that because they wanted to. It was not, "Boy, we really like him. Let's give him a raise." The guild negotiated a new contract. I thought I would be the richest guy in town.

I got hired in '68, and I was the first of nine guys who were hired by the St. Paul papers in the span of two and a half years. One of the last was Charley Hallman, the goofiest son of a gun I ever worked with in my life. Great guy. And Gary Olson too. We hired them on the same day, February 1, 1970. I always called it the Day of Infamy.

Later that year, in August, when I was just 24 or 25, the newsroom boss came to me and said, "Ken Murphy is going to retire in three years. We've got you targeted to be the morning sports editor." It was an extra 50 bucks if I got the job. Back then it was like, "Oh, 50 bucks a week? Sure, I'll take it!" About two months later, Murph died of a heart attack, in October of 1970.

The paper didn't know what to do. Murph was one of those 16-,

17-hours-a-day guys in the office. We had this crusty afternoon staff. Murph would come in in the morning about 10:30, and the afternoon staff would all take off. Somebody was supposed to wait around and read the paper, but they would all leave.

When Murph died, the *Dispatch* staff were all lamenting it, saying, "Oh geez, Murph. Nice guy." Mark Tierney, one of the veteran staffers, said, "Boys, the honeymoon is over."

Suddenly I became the most ill-equipped sports editor in the history of man.

Mike Augustin had been my boss in St. Cloud, and we got him down to St. Paul to cover the Gophers. We also had Jim Wells, another great guy. He submitted the most false résumé ever to get a job as a prep writer. He had been a copy boy in Arizona, and he convinced us that we were hiring a guy who had covered Arizona State or something. The remainder of the crew was Carl Peterson, Gregg Wong, Pat Thompson, and the great Chuck Dixon, plus Hallman and Olson.

Luigi's was a bar across the street from the newspaper offices. They would cash your check on payday every other Friday if you wanted. They'd have $80,000 on hand. You'd go in, cash your check, pay off your bar bill from the last two weeks, and take the remaining pittance home to your wife.

One night I wanted to take my wife at the time, Jean, to dinner. I was out of money. Luigi's gave me $50 and put it on my bar bill.

Everybody came to Luigi's to drink. Printers. Cops. Nurses from Miller Hospital. The night shifters would all drink there, and we'd call over at 12:45 AM to give them our order because we might not get there until 1:05 AM.

I used to work the slot, as the makeup editor, a lot of Saturdays. We had the early edition on Saturdays, with a 7 PM deadline. Then we didn't have to get another edition out until 10:30 PM.

About 7:30 I would announce to the staff, "Boys, it's time for the pre-crush cocktail." We'd all take a break and go over to Luigi's. Some nights, if I was distracted by work, a colleague would look at his watch and say, "Hey, Patrick, isn't it about time for the pre-crush cocktail?"

I started writing a Sunday column called "Reusse at Random." Each column would discuss three topics, and I would rip everybody, just crucify them. Readers think I can be a little harsh now, but I was a real jackass with "Random."

Back then, the Minneapolis papers had two sports staffs. When we traveled for games or tournaments, three beat writers would cover it, two from Minneapolis and one from St. Paul.

We viewed Minneapolis as the giant. The circulation areas were much more defined than they are today. The St. Paul papers were big in western Wisconsin and southeast Minnesota. Down toward Rochester and Winona, we competed with the Minneapolis papers, but anywhere west of the river we were nonexistent. From Minneapolis to the South Dakota border, we were invisible. Later on in my career, I would go outstate and write columns and people would say, "I've never seen the St. Paul paper."

When the Vikings went on the road, the *Tribune* would send their beat writer and Sid Hartman. The afternoon *Star* would send two reporters, their beat writer and another writer. We would send one guy, the great Ralphie Reeve. He would write two pieces for the morning paper and then the afternoon story. We did not send columnists anywhere.

Don Riley was our columnist for the morning edition. The column was billed as "The Eye Opener." Half of Riley's columns would lead "zim, zam, zoomie and zow." He would write stuff off the top of his head.

Riley was early on ripping Vince Lombardi and the Packers. He always referred to Green Bay as "Green Bush." One time in the early '70s, he wrote something like, "They're going to be coming by dogsled. They're going to come in fishing boats. The Green Bushers are coming to town." He wrote this whole thing about what a bunch of hillbillies they were. The mail from readers would come in by the box loads. He was a Twitter troller 50 years before Twitter. It was hilarious. He loved it.

Riley became famous enough that he would speak at high school athletic banquets. There probably wasn't a high school in western Wisconsin from Eau Claire to Superior where he didn't speak at a banquet. He would pick up $300, $400, and the crowd would boo him. He would tell the athletes how great they were and that they should move out of Wisconsin as soon as they could. But he was such a good-natured guy.

Riley was the first guy I knew who went to alcohol treatment. He was like the rest of us: he had a drinking problem. One time, he came roaring into the office on a Friday evening at about eight o'clock saying, "I'm late, I'm late." I said, "No, Don, you're 12 hours early." He thought it was morning.

He went to Bismarck, North Dakota, to sober up. It was a hard-nosed place. He was there for nine weeks. When he got back, I said to him, "Don, were you up there drying out or running for governor?" He was in treatment for a long time, but he stayed sober for the rest of his life. He became a salesman for sobriety.

Riley always had some moneymaking scam going, and they all failed miserably. He always had one for the state fair. He wanted to get in on that state fair bonanza. This was so long ago that chow mein was just becoming popular in Minnesota. He and his buddy came up with the "Chow Cone"—chow mein in a cone. They opened at 10 o'clock on the first Thursday of the fair, and at 10:10 a customer came up to buy a chow mein cone. As he walked away, the hot chow mein began leaking out of the bottom of the cone and got all over his clothes. Chow mein in a cone was not going to work, and they closed it down. And they had to give this guy $20 for dry cleaning.

One of my favorite Riley stories was one time when he went to Notre Dame to cover a football game. His wife, Dottie, went with him. She was a saint. On the way home, they stopped in Tomah in western Wisconsin to get gas. Dottie had been sleeping in the back seat, and she woke up to go to the restroom. Don got in the car after filling up the tank and drove all the way home to Roseville. Their daughters were sitting on the front steps when he got there. "Dad, you left Mom in Tomah." He took a big cup of coffee and drove all the way back to Tomah to get Dottie.

Another time, in 1972 (when he was still drinking), we sent him to a Notre Dame football game at the University of Southern California. It was the famous game where Anthony Davis scored six touchdowns for USC. In those days, reporters would give their copy to Western Union, and they'd send it into the paper by telex.

Don left for California on Thursday, and then we didn't see any copy on Friday, didn't see anything on Saturday, and didn't see anything on Sunday after the game was played. Sometime on Monday, we heard the telex machine going *ding, ding, ding, ding.* It was Don's story in advance of the game—48 hours after Anthony Davis had already scored his six touchdowns and led USC to a 45–23 win over Notre Dame, and Don was checking in with his advance. He was something.

■ ■ ■

I worked for the *St. Paul Pioneer Press* and *Dispatch* for almost 20 years, from September 1968 to June '88. I covered baseball for five years—as the Twins' beat guy from 1974 to '78—and then I started as a columnist in February 1979. Riley was still the morning guy, and I was the afternoon guy.

As a glorious introduction to my new role, the headline across the top of the *Dispatch*'s front page read: "Column by Pat Ruesse Debuts Today."

They had my name spelled wrong—and I had been there 10 years.

4

MY FIRST LOVE: BASEBALL

The Baseball Writers' Association of America (BBWAA) issues cards to media members who belong to the organization and regularly cover baseball. Each card has a number that denotes a person's seniority in the BBWAA, No. 1 being the longest active member. As of 2022, Reusse stands at No. 6 on the seniority list.

Reusse has been nominated three times for what was long known as the J. G. Taylor Spink Award, which is baseball writing's highest honor. Winners are celebrated annually at the Hall of Fame ceremony in Cooperstown, New York.

■ ■ ■

The Twins coming to the Twin Cities in 1961 was the greatest thing to ever happen to me as a sports fan. My five years covering the Twins were also five of my most enjoyable years as a sportswriter.

I became the baseball beat writer for the St. Paul papers starting in late 1973. Bob Fowler had been the Twins beat guy, but he left and went to the *Minneapolis Star*.

The first thing I covered as the beat writer was the winter meetings in Houston. I realized right away that winter meetings and a fondness for alcohol don't mix well. I was a neophyte. I knew some baseball writers at the time, and all those guys soon became my

< 37 >

buddies. The best sportswriting friends I have nationally today are old ball writers from those days.

I was still on the beat when owner Calvin Griffith made his infamous speech at the Waseca Lions Club in southern Minnesota. It was near the end of the 1978 season, and I was in Kansas City covering the Twins' final series. The story broke on Sunday morning. Rod Carew went nuts in the clubhouse when he heard what Calvin had said.

Nick Coleman, a *Star Tribune* reporter at the time, was in Waseca visiting his in-laws. His father-in-law said, "Want to go listen to Calvin? He's speaking to the Lions Club." Coleman could never have known what he was walking into.

Calvin had some drinks in him, and he got some laughs early, so he kept on rolling. According to Coleman's article, Griffith was asked why he had decided to move the team from Washington to Minnesota back in '61. He said: "I'll tell you why we came to Minnesota. It was when I found out you only had 15,000 blacks here. Black people don't go to ball games, but they'll fill up a rassling ring and put up such a chant it'll scare you to death. It's unbelievable. We came here because you've got good, hardworking, white people here."

Obviously, those racist comments are what stuck out, but Calvin said some other poorly considered things that night. Among them were his comments about former Twins infielder Jerry Terrell. Terrell was from Elysian, Minnesota, just five miles from Waseca, and he went to Waseca High School. He was a plucky infielder who somehow stuck around in the majors for eight years, including five with the Twins. Someone in the crowd at the Lions Club that night asked Calvin what he thought of Terrell. Calvin said, "It's a disgrace that a guy with his talent is in the big leagues." I mean, that's how PR conscious Calvin was.

The story lived for about a month. In modern times, if that story ran on Sunday, Calvin would have been removed by noon Monday.

I was in Kansas City working the clubhouse after the story appeared in the *Tribune*. Rodney went bonkers and said he would not play for Calvin again. And he was right. Four months later, the future Hall of Famer was traded to the California Angels.

Calvin displayed his willingness to speak his mind on other occasions as well. On September 30, 1981, the Twins played their last game at Met Stadium in Bloomington. Only about 13,000 people showed up, and 10,000 of those in attendance were rowdy college kids. It was just a crazy crowd. The team was going to remove home plate during a postgame ceremony. Calvin wasn't out there on the field. He was in the pressroom. The whole crowd started chanting, "Cal-vin, Cal-vin, Cal-vin."

It was the last day at Met Stadium, the fans were chanting for him, and Calvin finally came out. He headed for the microphone and said, "If you people had showed up for more games, we wouldn't have to be moving downtown." He just ripped them.

Despite all that, Calvin knew a baseball player when he saw one. Calvin told manager Sam Mele in '67, "Rod Carew is your second baseman." Carew was just 21 at the time and had only played A ball. Mele brought in the beat writers and said, "I just want you to know this is not my decision. This is coming from Calvin—that we're going to play this kid." Rodney went on to win the 1967 American League Rookie of the Year Award.

■ ■ ■

When I started on the Twins beat in '74, the Twins were a mix of fading veterans nearing the end of their careers, like Tony Oliva and Harmon Killebrew; budding stars like Carew, Larry Hisle, and Bert Blyleven; and a bunch of scrappers. They also had the cheapest payroll and lowest attendance in the American League.

Danny Thompson was the shortstop. One of the greatest guys ever. Before the '73 season, when he was just 26 years old, Danny was diagnosed with leukemia—back when it was pretty much a death sentence. During the baseball season, he would go to the Mayo Clinic on days off for experimental treatments and come back with huge sores on his arms from the injections. Early in '76 he wasn't playing very well, and Calvin said, "I don't know; there must be something on his mind." The master of PR strikes again.

On June 1, 1976, Thompson was traded along with Blyleven to Texas. The Rangers came to town for a two-game series in late September, with Danny as the starting shortstop. He passed away just a few months later, on December 10, 1976, at the age of 29.

Thompson's double-play partner in '76 was the rookie second baseman Bob Randall. Bobby was from Gove, Kansas. Thompson was from tiny Capron, Oklahoma. I called them the "Sod Brothers." They both played the same way: always hustling and diving on their bellies. Randall would get killed turning double plays, but he'd hang in there.

Bobby gave me a great quote. His senior class at Gove was just four boys. He made this observation: "The senior prom was a bummer."

The Twins started the '74 season in Kansas City. They won the Friday-night opener, 6–4. Next day, they got beat 23–6. Bill Hands started that game and was lucky to get out with his life. The Sunday game was rained out, so the Twins split the series.

They went back to Kansas City for a four-game series in August. Remember, this is the Royals with George Brett and Hal McRae and those guys, just hitting the ball into the gaps at Royals Stadium—with its fast turf, like a racetrack. The Twins have no chance. They gave up 17 runs in the series opener—meaning they gave up 40 runs in 16 innings in consecutive games in KC.

One of the Twins' starters in '74 was a lefty named Vic Albury. "Fast Victor" I called him. He came in to relieve starter Ray Corbin in the third inning of the 17–3 thrashing by the Royals. He pitched five innings in relief that night and gave up 10 runs. He called the press box to complain that only nine of them should have been earned.

A couple of years later, in '76, I was traveling with the Twins to New Orleans for a three-game exhibition series against the Houston Astros in what were the first baseball games ever played in the

Superdome. As the bus came into town at night, the roof of the Superdome appeared bright white before us. Bert Blyleven hooted from the back of the bus, "God, it looks like Albury's fastball."

The Twins were a screwed-up operation, but the characters made covering it fun.

■ ■ ■

Frank Quilici was the manager when I got on the Twins beat. He had been the third base coach under manager Bill Rigney until the team fired Rigney halfway through the '72 season. Before Rigney, Billy Martin had lasted one season as manager, in 1969. He won 97 games that year and won the American League West Division, but the team fired Martin because he drank too much and liked to punch people.

Howard Fox was the team's traveling secretary then; as Joe Soucheray once wrote, "He put the mint on Calvin's pillow when they were on the road." Martin and Fox hated each other. Fox would hand out the hotel room keys when they got to a new city on road trips. One night in Baltimore—this was back when Martin was the third base coach—Billy was anxious to get to the bar or something, and Howard took too long to give Billy his key. So Billy punched him. Later, when the team was considering hiring Billy as manager, Howard fought against it like crazy.

When the team fired Billy Martin, a lot of Minnesota baseball fans swore they would never go to another Twins game. Why people loved that doofus, I could never understand. He was one of the worst guys I ever met in sports, but the fans loved him because he was fiery and would get thrown out of games.

The Twins won the division again in Rigney's first year, 1970, but they slipped to fifth place the next season, and then the team fired him in '72. Not only had the wins declined, but attendance had fallen off a cliff. Calvin hired Quilici and said, "I guess the fans wanted an Italian"—like Martin.

Quilici was the manager my first two years on the beat, '74 and

'75. In both those years he had a three-person coaching staff—which tells you how low-budget the operation was. Then Quilici was fired and the team hired Gene Mauch to manage in '76.

Mauch had been the manager of the Minneapolis Millers in the late '50s when the team was really good, and so he was well known around town. He had Sid Hartman on his side too. Mauch had been managing in the majors since 1960, with the Phillies and the Expos.

Mauch was the greatest thing that ever happened to me as a baseball writer. Fowler and I would go out to dinner with Mauch on the road some Saturday nights. One thing I learned from him is that you never mention the social gatherings to anyone. If you went out drinking with a manager, the next day you acted as if you hadn't seen him since you were at the ballpark the day before.

The other thing I learned from covering Mauch was that with certain guys you wait to get the answer. Don't get antsy. If you asked Mauch a question, he would take the time to think of an answer. Sometimes it took 20, 30 seconds, but then it would be good.

I was the only guy on the road with the Twins in Milwaukee late in the 1979 season. Mauch and I went out for a few drinks and then dinner at Sally's Steak House. He took out his official umpire evaluation card. His rankings were 1 for good, 2 for fair, 3 for poor. Durwood Merrill was a young umpire at the time. In the attitude category, Mauch gave Merrill a 7—off the chart. Gene was an open book when he wasn't at the ballpark.

In Mauch's first season, in '76, the Twins finished in third place with a record of 85–77. The next season was about the same, 84–77. That team had a hell of a lineup. They had Larry Hisle, Lyman Bostock, and Rod Carew. They scored 867 runs—the most in the major leagues that year—without hitting a lot of home runs (123). They just couldn't pitch.

The game against the Chicago White Sox on June 26 that year was legendary. It was a beautiful Sunday afternoon. The Twins won a 19–12 shoot-out at Met Stadium. Right fielder Glenn Adams drove in eight runs for the Twins. "Hit-and-bitch" we called him, because he could hit and he could bitch.

That day Rodney went 4-for-5, with a double and a homer, and got his batting average up to .403. It was the Twins' biggest regular-season crowd in Met Stadium history (46,463). The fans gave Rodney roughly nine standing ovations.

The next weekend, the Twins traveled to Chicago for a four-game series. They got swept. In the Sunday doubleheader, the Twins lost the first game when Danny Ford forgot to wear his sunglasses in right field and allowed a winning White Sox rally by losing a ball in the sun. Disco Dan is one of my favorite humans, but the guy is from a different planet.

The Twins clubhouse was open between the games. I was going to the clubhouse, but not to talk to Mauch. I knew he was going to be in no mood to answer questions. Bob Greenberg was a radio announcer in Chicago at the time, and he was blind. I heard him say to the guy with him, "Maybe we should go in and see Gene." I stood in front of the door and said, "I just want to assist you gentlemen and say this would not be a good time to go in and see manager Mauch. You might want to try some of the fellas out in the clubhouse." That wouldn't have looked good as a headline: "Mauch Punches Unsighted Radio Announcer."

Mauch always had a postgame cocktail and a cigarette. At Met Stadium the game would end, and I'd send in my early story to the paper, go down the elevator, and walk along the corridor toward the clubhouse. It took about five minutes to get to the clubhouse. Sometimes I'd get to Mauch's office and see the uniform sitting in a pile in the middle of the room and I could almost see smoke rising above it. Then I'd know, *No Gene quotes today!*

That was the case following a game in 1978 involving another incident with Disco Dan Ford. The Twins were playing the White Sox in early September. They were down 4–0 in the bottom of the seventh but had the bases loaded, with designated hitter José Morales on second and Ford on third. Bombo Rivera got a hit to center field, and Disco Dan started jogging home. José was right behind him.

As he got close to home plate, Disco Dan turned around and started waving José in. José crossed the plate triumphantly, seemingly cutting the Twins' deficit to 4–2. Then it was revealed that Disco Dan had not yet touched home plate. He was so busy cheering and waving that he forgot to touch the plate, which caused Morales to be called out for passing Disco on the bases. That killed a Twins rally in what ended as a 4–3 loss.

Joe Brinkman was the home plate umpire that night. A former star running back at Holdingford High School in central Minnesota, Brinkman went on to spend 35 years as a major league umpire, but this was still relatively early in his career.

Mauch started walking toward Brinkman at home plate as Ford was walking toward the dugout, head down. Mauch said to Ford, "Leave!" That's all he said: "Leave!" Meaning, leave the stadium.

Mauch went up to Brinkman and said, "'Did what I think happened just happen?" And Brinkman replied, "Yep."

I don't know if we got quotes from Gene after that game, but I'm guessing that was a night when his uniform was sitting in a pile.

Mauch took losses terribly. There were some memorable postgame press conferences earlier in his career when he dumped over the buffet table in the middle of the clubhouse. One night after a loss with the Twins, Mauch was taking angry laps around the clubhouse, waiting to see if anyone would have the audacity to head to the buffet table. Suddenly, he saw a figure moving toward the food. He turned and saw that it was Carew, and he headed back to his office.

My best Mauch moment came in '76. He had been the manager of the Philadelphia Phillies in 1964 when they lost 10 games in a row and blew the National League pennant in the final week of the season. He was given full blame for that collapse.

In 1976 Mauch was the new Twins manager, and the Phillies had built a 15-game lead in the NL East Division by late August.

Their lead was down to four games within a couple of weeks. The "Fading Phillies" were back in the headlines.

Around this time, I was at Met Stadium for early batting practice before a game. Gene was standing in front of the dugout, smoking a cigarette, watching the Twins practice. I walked up to him and started with a little small talk. "Hey, Gene. How ya doing?" Blah, blah, blah. Finally, after a few minutes, I asked, "What do you remember about '64?"

Ten seconds go by, 20 seconds, 30 seconds, 40 seconds. I thought this was a question he wasn't actually going to answer.

Then he threw his cigarette down in the grass, crunched it, and said, "Only every [bleeping] pitch."

He went on for another 40 minutes. It was unbelievable. If I didn't get along with him, I'm sure he would have told me the same thing he told Disco Dan: *Leave!*

■ ■ ■

The Twins under Calvin Griffith were notoriously cheap, but they had the best hospitality room in baseball. It was called the Twins Room. Nice meals before games. Scouts, some club officials, and writers would be in there. Jimmy Robertson, one of Calvin's brothers, ran the Twins Room. After night games, he'd head out at about one o'clock in the morning and say, "Lock the door when you leave, boys." We'd be in there until three in the morning on occasion. We'd talk about life and drink and tell stories . . . and drink.

There were rumors around this time that the Twins were going to relocate to Seattle as part of a lawsuit settlement. Seattle had the expansion Pilots for one year (1969) before the franchise moved to Milwaukee and became the Brewers. The city of Seattle had filed suit against the American League. That was the first "Twins are leaving" rumor. The team won 82 games in '74, but their attendance was terrible—worst in the American League.

They lost a doubleheader to Oakland in June of 1975, and I

wrote that it was a two-act play that could be called "Death of a Franchise"—a play on *Death of a Salesman*. It was kind of harmless, I thought. "A's Star in Death of Franchise" was the big headline in the next day's sports section.

The Twins were furious, to the point that they put up a sign in the pressroom that said, "Twins Room closes one hour after the game." They were going to hit me where it hurt: free food and drink.

The California Angels had a trio of beat writers who were full-scale running mates: Dick Miller, Don Merry, and John Stellman. They were at the Met with the Angels a couple of weeks later, saw the sign, and lit it on fire. Burned it off the wall. They weren't leaving after an hour. The Twins Room was back in business.

The bartender in the Twins Room was an old Irishman named Art Ruane. Later he got a job as a security guard at the Schmidt Brewery, and I wrote a column about him. I said hiring Art Ruane at a brewery was like putting a pyromaniac in charge of an oil refinery. He had a bad leg and was 70 years old.

Artie would serve drinks before the game, and then he would sit in the Twins Room during the game, drinking beer and getting belligerent. Angels manager Jim Fregosi was in there one night, and Artie said, "Little Jimmy Fregosi. Couldn't take a step to his right at shortstop," referring to Fregosi's playing career. I mean, he ripped everybody.

Artie had a lot of strong opinions. At least twice a week he did or said something that would have gotten him fired from pretty much any other job. But we loved him because he was such a character.

I was in the Twins Room late one night after a game in 1980. It was about two in the morning. Frank Quilici, who was working as an announcer by then, was there; I had never seen him there that late before. Bill Mazeroski, who was a coach for Seattle at the time, was also there, as was Mike Robertson, the Twins' traveling secretary.

Artie started telling Mazeroski what a fraud he was, that he couldn't turn the double play. Artie was the world's No. 1 proponent of the double play. A self-proclaimed expert on it. Keep in mind, Maz made it into the Hall of Fame (in 2001) largely on his ability to turn the double play.

Artie's going on and on at Mazeroski. Finally, we got an idea. We told Artie, with his stiff leg, to show Maz the proper way to turn a double play.

The room wasn't big, and we moved all the furniture out of the way. We put a towel down for second base. We got a glove on Artie. Quilici was the shortstop. He was going to toss the ball to Art, and Art was going to gracefully come across second base and make an accurate throw to first. Mazeroski was the base runner, standing about 25 feet away.

Robertson smacked his hand to signal the ball being hit, and here comes Mazeroski. He slid like a real base runner across the rug, got Artie in his bad leg, and knocked him in the air. The ball rolled across the floor. The glove was on the floor. Artie's glasses were askew on his head. Artie looked up at Mazeroski and said, "I told you I could turn the double play."

At some ballparks, they'd have drinks in the press box during the game. At Arlington Stadium in Texas, they started serving alcohol in the second inning. Waitresses would come and ask if you wanted a drink. *Uh, yes, I will have one.* One time when I was on the road with the Twins in Texas, there was a two-hour rain delay in the middle of the game. We ended up drinking a lot. When I got back to town, I looked up my story of the game. It was unfamiliar, but it actually wasn't that bad.

Later that night we were flying into Detroit, and it was taking forever. Bob Fowler was sitting next to me. Steve Braun was sitting in front of us. I loved Braun, a left-handed hitter who played both infield and outfield.

I decided to have a little fun with Fowler. I said to Steve, "Braunie, the biggest fraud in history is all these old-time legendary ballplayers. You're a better hitter than Ty Cobb ever dreamt of being."

This got Fowler going. He asked me, "Who's better, [Twins catcher] Glenn Borgmann or [Hall of Famer] Gabby Hartnett?"

I said, "Glenn Borgmann. No contest."

So we do this whole routine. You know, me saying that Blyleven is better than Walter Johnson, and so on.

Then he said, "Honus Wagner or Sergio Ferrer?"

Sergio—who would have a short major league career—was sitting right there. I said, "I'll have to think about that one."

Poor Sergio.

■ ■ ■

I covered the Twins as a beat writer for only five years, but baseball was always my No. 1 love. The World Series wins in '87 and '91 were hard to beat during my 50-plus years as a sports reporter and columnist.

The win in '91 is the greatest event in Minnesota sports history, but the first championship in '87 was the one that people really went psychotic for. It was just so unlikely. The '91 team was legitimately good, winning 95 games, and the Toronto team they beat in the AL Championship Series was the toughest opponent either of those Twins teams had to face.

The '87 Minnesota Twins, meanwhile, are the only team in baseball history to be outscored during the regular season and go on to win the World Series. They finished with just 85 wins, and they couldn't buy a road win—they went 29–52 away from the Dome. Dennis Brackin, the beat writer for the *Star Tribune* at the time, suggested that the team bring in a hypnotist to cure them of their road woes. Brackin always was after the goofy angle.

At the start of a road trip to Milwaukee late in '87, Brackin told me he'd talked to a hypnotist named Harvey Misel, and he was going to ask manager Tom Kelly about it. I said, "Jesus Christ. Wait until the end of the road trip. Whatever you do, don't break that idea out tonight in Milwaukee."

The team was terrible on the road, and Brackin was going to

suggest that Harvey would hypnotize the players and make them better. That was not going to play well with old Jay Thomas Kelly.

If you got TK in a bad mood, it could last for days. Still, right out of the chute, Brackin asked him about the hypnotist. Harvey had gotten some fame when Carew used him 10 years earlier to help Rod clear whatever issue was on his mind at the time.

That angle had no chance. TK was grumpy enough watching his team play poorly on the road, and then Brackin was saying, *Let's hypnotize them.* Bad idea.

Despite the team's troubles winning road games, TK held the '87 squad together well enough for them to stay in first place uninterrupted from early June through the end of the year. This was just TK's second full season as a major league skipper, but he had worked with many of the players when he was managing in the instructional league or at Class AA Orlando. They were his guys, and they were some characters.

There was a room in the Metrodome clubhouse next to the manager's office that had several trunks in it. Gary Gaetti and Kent Hrbek would go in that room after every game. If you were looking for them for a quote, you could probably find them in there sipping a little Wild Turkey and smoking cigarettes for about 45 minutes.

And Kirby Puckett—I never saw a guy who could stir up a clubhouse as rapidly as he could. This was even true during spring training. He was such a good guy as a teammate that players with No. 88 on their backs in spring training could tell Puck that he was short and fat, and he didn't care—he treated everyone the same. The team could be coming off of five losses in a row, and Puck would be shouting in the locker room, "Don't worry about this one, boys. I'm going to win this one for us today. You guys take care of tomorrow."

Still, no one ever imagined that this team was going to win the World Series. The day we knew for certain that the Twins, and not the Vikings, would be the main topic of conversation that fall was during the Twins' last home game on Sunday, September 27. More than 50,000 fans were on hand at the Metrodome that afternoon to watch the Twins play Kansas City. In the top of the first inning, second baseman Al Newman started a 5–4–2 double play to stifle an early Royals rally. The crowd went insane. The Twins came back and scored five runs in the bottom of the first on the way to an 8–1 win. And that's when we knew they were going to win the division.

The team gets some heat for its relatively unimpressive final record (85–77), but they lost the last five games after clinching the division. They were nearly a 90-win team. And the best baseball they ever played was during the five games against the Detroit Tigers in the American League Championship Series.

The Tigers won 98 games that season, but they were old and a bit worn out from battling Toronto to the finish to win the East Division. I wrote a column predicting that the Tigers would win the ALCS in five games. Then, after the Twins won the first two games of the series at home, I wrote, "I didn't say which five." Then the Twins lost Game 3 in Detroit, and I wrote that they were going to win this series because they played great in Tiger Stadium, losing 7–6 after Detroit scored twice in the bottom of the eighth.

Roy Smalley came up to me before Game 4 and said, "That was quite a desperate leap for our bandwagon. You just made it by your fingernails."

He was right. The Twins kept playing great and won the next two and were on to the World Series for the first time since 1965, with a chance to claim the franchise's first world championship since the Washington Senators in 1924.

Calvin Griffith had sold the team to Carl Pohlad in 1984, but he was in Detroit for the ALCS and was standing outside the clubhouse after Game 5. As reporters waited to get access to the winning Twins players, I went over to congratulate Calvin. (He had signed most of the guys on the team.) That's when he told me about being the bat boy for the '24 Senators, who were owned by his uncle, Clark Griffith. Calvin said the fans stormed the field after the win and took all the batting practice balls. He was crying after the game because the shag bag was empty. Clark said, "Calvin, today that's OK. We won the World Series."

I was working for the St. Paul paper, and we had five, six guys covering the ALCS. As we were sitting up there in the Tiger Stadium press box hacking away, we heard a report that the welcome home reception for the team had been moved from the airport to the Metrodome. They might have 10,000 people. Then they might have 20,000. We were still hacking away when we heard that there were 50,000 people waiting for the team inside the Dome. I looked up and said, "Fellas, I think we're in the wrong place."

All the players say that was the most amazing moment, arriving at the Dome after beating Detroit—even more so than winning the World Series and the parade that followed. It was a team with a whole lot of crazy stuff going on, and the fans loved it.

The 1991 World Series had the best games, but '87 was the greatest reaction we've ever had. The parade was insane. There were people hanging out of buildings.

There was nothing about the Carl Pohlad operation originally that made you think they were an upgrade over the Griffith organization. But Carl made some key decisions that put the team on a path to win. First, he hired Andy MacPhail to be the general manager in 1985. MacPhail then gave Tom Kelly the managerial job in '86. And then, before the '87 season—when they needed a closer, and they needed a left fielder and leadoff hitter—they went out and acquired Jeff Reardon and Dan Gladden.

Somehow the team pieced it together despite a somewhat suspect pitching staff. Blyleven and Frank Viola were quality number one and two starters, but Les Straker—who had a lifetime record of 10–15—was the No. 3 guy. And Juan Berenguer and Dan Schatzeder were competent setup guys for Reardon in the bullpen. But overall, the team had one of the worst ERAs in the league.

In addition to some big bats in Puckett, Hrbek, Gaetti, and Tom Brunansky, they also were a great fielding team. Herbie was a great first baseman. Steve Lombardozzi was a very good second baseman. Greg Gagne is the best shortstop the team has ever had.

Gaetti is the best third baseman they've ever had. Puckett in center field was young and could cover a lot of ground. Gladdy in left and Bruno in right, and Randy Bush was a hell of a good extra player.

They were just so thin with the pitching that you wondered how they were going to win. But somehow they did—and produced one of the greatest moments in Minnesota sports history.

5

THE CHARACTERS ARE WHAT MADE THE GAME FUN

The charm of baseball that maintains a magnetic pull on Reusse goes beyond the daily rhythm of summer, in-game strategy ripe for second-guessing, or the beauty of box scores. It's the people involved, the true characters who can be extraordinarily talented or savvy on the field but also certifiably goofy or hilarious off the field. Reusse has encountered many who fit both categories in the world of baseball.

■ ■ ■

Lyman Bostock is one of my all-time favorites. He was the greatest talker of all time. They called him "Jibber Jabber." He came up in '75, although he missed a chunk of the season after he injured himself running full speed into the wall in Oakland. In '77 he was a monster as a two-way player and ended up hitting .336, second only to teammate Rod Carew in the American League. Bostock was going to be a free agent after the season, and his future seemed bright.

In the middle of the '77 season, the Twins were in Anaheim to play the Angels. I didn't make the trip, and the St. Paul paper didn't send anyone out to cover the series. Lyman talked to someone

< 53 >

from the *Los Angeles Times* while he was there, and he ripped the Twins. Ripped Minnesota as a baseball market. He thought he was just talking to LA—what difference could it make? The *Pioneer Press* had the *LA Times–Chicago Tribune* newswire, so the display story in the morning paper was Bostock's LA interview.

The Twins traveled back to Minnesota on the red-eye and arrived at 5:30 in the morning. Lyman picked up the paper at the airport and saw the headline, "Bostock Rips Twins." He was in a panic because he was a very sensitive kid. If the fans were going to boo him, he would take it very hard.

I got a phone call at home. I don't know how he had my number, but when I answered he said, "Poison"—that's what he called me—"you've got to help me out here. I didn't say all these things." I told him, "Yes, you did, Lyman, but what do you want to tell me?" He backtracked and gave me a quote—"I think the fans are great," he said—and I wrote it for the afternoon *Dispatch*.

After the season he signed with the Angels, and he got off to a lousy start in '78. So he donated his first month's salary to charity. The Angels were in Minnesota for a two-game series late in the season. I went down to the clubhouse after the second game to say goodbye to him. He said, "You take it easy on my boys, Poison." A few minutes later, I was coming out of the Twins clubhouse and he was leaving the visitors' clubhouse. I gave him a big ol' wave, and he yelled, "See you later, Poison."

The Angels then traveled to Chicago for a weekend series with the White Sox. Lyman went to visit relatives in Gary, Indiana, which he always did when he was in the Chicago area. On Saturday night, he was murdered in a case of jealous rage. He was only 27 years old.

It was awful. Awful.

■ ■ ■

If you were around in 1977, watching Bostock with Carew and Larry Hisle, you can't forget the rivalry between that run-scoring machine and Bill Veeck's South Side Hit Men in Chicago. Both squads had powerful lineups that summer, but with free agency about to take over baseball, these two underfinanced teams would not be able to hold on to their top players much longer.

Veeck was an all-time character and a genius promoter with a wooden peg leg. He was the White Sox owner, and the South Side was jumping that year. The old Comiskey Park was my favorite ballpark. The sightlines were great. When it was full, the place was nuts, and Nancy Faust was incredible on the organ.

There was a big fight in front of the press box one day. Veeck decided to go down and break it up. Next thing you saw was that peg leg of his sticking straight up in the air.

When the Saints started in St. Paul, I gave Mike Veeck—Bill's son and the Saints' owner—a lot of grief. Everybody thought I must have hated his old man, but I loved his old man. Veeck sold the White Sox in 1981, and he went to Wrigley Field all the time after that to watch the Cubs, which is where he had gotten his start in baseball. I arranged to sit with him in the Wrigley bleachers one afternoon. It was a beautiful sunny day. He was sitting there in shorts and no shirt. He could drink more beer than anybody I ever saw. I remember writing in a column about that day, "One of his legs was tan and the other was varnished."

■ ■ ■

Bert Blyleven was another major character on the Twins when I started covering them. Bert and I always had an interesting relationship. He saw me as siding with Calvin Griffith on labor issues, which created some tension between us. I also did not give him proper credit for how good he was and how little run support he got from the Twins' lineup. During his first tenure with the team (1970–76), Bert consistently ranked among the league leaders in ERA, but his win-loss record was just 99–90. In '73 he was second in the league in ERA and had the fifth-most losses.

Howard Fox always loved Blyleven. He thought letting Bert go was the worst mistake the Twins ever made, and he might have been right. But the team was never going to pay his freight.

Bert was traded to the Texas Rangers in June 1976. In the last game he pitched for Minnesota that season, he gave a dismissive gesture—emphatically raising his right arm and then grabbing his forearm—in the direction of the owner's booth as he was coming off the field. Calvin was in Orlando at the time, but Bert thought he was in his booth. Bert knew he was getting traded, and he wanted to give Calvin a proper send-off.

After the game, the writers gathered around Blyleven in the locker room for an interview. Bert said, "There are two fat guys I'm not going to miss in this town: Calvin and that one." He pointed at me.

Then the first time I was in Texas when he was pitching for them—well, in modern times this would have been a story, but as sportswriters we weren't as sensitive back then.

The old Texas ballpark, Arlington Stadium, was a dump. To get to the visiting clubhouse, you had to either walk under the bleachers and hope you didn't run into a snake or go on the field along the left-field line. I took the latter path and was walking down the field when, all of a sudden, these baseballs came flying at me. I took one in the back. It was Bert, who was out collecting balls by the mound during batting practice. After he hit me in the back, I looked over and said, "I hope that was a curveball."

After Texas, Bert went to pitch for Pittsburgh and then Cleveland. Barely two weeks after he pitched in the '85 All-Star Game, Cleveland traded him to Minnesota for a bunch of prospects.

When Bert came back, our relationship was OK. Most of the time.

In '86, his first full season back, he gave up 50 home runs—a record that still stands in 2022. He also had a streak of home runs in consecutive games. One afternoon at the Dome, he had avoided giving up a homer until late in the game, when a high fly ball settled in behind the plexiglass. I wrote the story from a celebratory point of view, like all day the tension had been building about whether he could do it and keep the streak going.

I showed up to the ballpark the next day and was sitting in the dugout watching batting practice. Bert came up to me and said, "You know, I tried to get along with you. But you're just an asshole." I said, "Bert, I knew you were going to react like that, but it was too good to pass up. Sorry."

When he tried to come back to the Twins for a third time, I was the only guy he knew at spring training. We were friendly then, but he didn't make the team.

I must point out that I always voted for Blyleven for Hall of Fame. There's no question he's a Hall of Famer.

■ ■ ■

I covered Tony Oliva for only two years as a player—'74 and '75— but he was a coach for the rest of my time on the Twins beat and beyond. Tony is one of the greatest human beings you'll ever meet, and December 5, 2021, when the Baseball Hall of Fame Veterans Committee voted both Oliva and longtime Twins pitcher Jim Kaat into the Hall of Fame, was a happy day for Minnesota baseball fans of every generation. For sure, Tony is the only guy with a plaque in Cooperstown who can give some credit to the failed 1961 Bay of Pigs invasion for him making it that far.

The Griffith-owned Washington Senators were the top recruiters of Cuban ballplayers in the 1950s, with standouts such as Camilo Pascual, Pedro Ramos, Zoilo Versalles, and a few others already on the roster when the team arrived from Washington. A guy named Papa Joe Cambria, who owned a restaurant in Baltimore, would spend the winters in Cuba and scrounge up baseball players for the Senators.

Cuba used to be wide open, but after Fidel Castro came to power in '59, Cubans couldn't go directly to the United States. Cambria signed his last batch of post-Castro ballplayers for the transplanted Twins in March 1961. Tony and another 20 Cuban players had to wait in Mexico for two weeks before they could fly to the United States.

It was early April before they arrived at the Twins minor league camp in Fernandina Beach, Florida. The rosters for the full-season minor league teams were already filled by then, so there weren't many jobs remaining.

The Twins staff watched Tony. They could see that he could hit, but he couldn't play the outfield. He was there a little more than a week, and then they told him to go home. But the Bay of Pigs incident had just occurred, preventing him from returning to Castro's Cuba. Tony knew a Cuban player on the Twins' single-A team in Charlotte, Minnie Mendoza, so he arranged to stay with him and work out there.

The organization decided to send Tony to the rookie league team in Wytheville, Virginia. Tony went there and batted .410.

He stayed in the minors for two more years and had a couple cups of coffee with the big-league club in '62 and '63 before making the Twins roster at spring training in '64. That year, he became the first American League rookie ever to win a batting title. And he won the batting title again the next year.

Tony started off the '64 season hitting 9 for 19, and then the team went to Detroit for a Sunday doubleheader. It was one of the rare TV games we got to see in Fulda. Phil Regan was the starting pitcher for Detroit in the opener. When Tony came up to bat in the first, Regan threw a fastball right at his head and sent him sprawling to the ground in the batter's box. I can still see it in my mind. Next pitch, Tony hit it over the head of Tigers center fielder Don Demeter for another base hit. He was a guy who wasn't going to be intimidated.

Tony's arrival coincided with Harmon Killebrew, the Twins' first hero, being in his prime as the American League's premier power hitter. Arno Goethel, the baseball writer for the *Pioneer Press*, labeled it the "KO Punch"—and they batted third or fourth in the lineup for seven years and were a perfect complement to each other. We called Harmon the "Killer" here in Minnesota, but the greatest nickname for him could be found in Jim Bouton's amazing baseball diary, *Ball Four*. Bouton was teammates with lefty Fritz Peterson on the Yankees. Bouton wrote that he'd see Peterson come into the clubhouse after pitching against the Twins and ask, "How'd you do, Fritz?" and Peterson would reply, "The Fat Kid hit a double with the bases loaded."

In Peterson's lingo, the Fat Kid was Killebrew. And here in Minnesota, he was our beloved Fat Kid, hitting baseballs to places we could barely imagine at Met Stadium. It was fantastic power to go with Tony's phenomenal hitting.

Tony would have been a 3,000-hit guy, easy, if it weren't for his knee problems. He had already had knee injuries and gone through some cleanup surgeries when he dived for a ball in Oakland in 1971 and landed on a sprinkler head with his right knee, and that ruined him. He was hitting .375 at the time, and although he limped on to nab his third batting title, at .337, he was never the same after that.

He played only 10 games in '72, and his career most likely would have been done if the designated hitter didn't come into the league in '73. He had a good year in '73 playing on one leg. In '74 he was OK, but in '75 he was cooked. In his final season of '76 he made only 128 plate appearances and hit .211. His playing career was officially over at age 37.

For 15 years, beginning with his first year of eligibility in 1982, Tony fell short in the annual voting for the Baseball Hall of Fame. His career stats missed some of those key markers that often ensure enshrinement—3,000 hits, 300 homers—but finally, in December 2021, he made it.

I always got along with Tony, and I can think of only one time when I got crossways with him. I had gotten into the Tanqueray's. We were on a flight coming back from Oakland. Somewhere over Sioux Falls the plane started rocking and rolling. Terrible turbulence. Tony hated flying even when it was smooth.

I yelled over to him, "Hey, Señor, at least you'll get your name in the first paragraph. I won't even get a mention if this thing crashes." Tony's response: "Don't you funny me, big man."

Tony had no enemies. In 2021 the Twins honored the '91 World Series team, and Tony got as big an ovation as anybody when he was introduced with the coaching staff. As his wife, Gordette, said, "Who doesn't like Tony?"

When Rodney Carew came along in 1967, he roomed with Tony on the road. When Tony became a coach after he stopped playing, he was able to have his own room. After about a year, he exercised that right, which upset Rodney.

Rodney is the biggest perfectionist of all time. I went to his batting cage out in Anaheim after he retired. It had a pebble surface. Here he is, the Hall of Famer, one of the greatest hitters ever, going through and picking up pebbles that are a little too large.

His first wife, Marilynn, and I became buddies. She told me about his sweater collection. She said that when he finds a sweater he likes, he buys five of them in different colors. He always wore sweaters, except in the summer. He would arrange his sweaters by color. The rows of sweaters had to match horizontally. In other words, the brown sweater had to be second in the piles all the way across the closet, the blues third, and so on. He's persnickety.

I took him out to breakfast once to do a column on him in the off-season. We ate at the beloved Lincoln Del restaurant in St. Louis Park. He sent his omelet back like four times. It was too fluffy, then it wasn't fluffy enough. He wasn't trying to be a pain in the ass. It was just him.

Rodney's uniform was always immaculate too, which is interesting because he chewed tobacco. He said the tobacco helped him hit. He would have a big wad in his right cheek, and he said it helped him open his eye wider.

Hitting was so routine for Rodney. His '77 season was the best one I've ever covered for any athlete. I mean, look at those numbers: .388 average, 100 RBIs, 14 home runs, 128 runs scored, plus 16 triples and 23 stolen bases. He was on the cover of *Time* magazine and *Sports Illustrated* the same week in July. After the season, he won the league MVP award handily.

Calvin gave him a $100,000 bonus at the end of the year. Then, of course, the following year Calvin got the Dubonnet in him in Waseca, and that ended the honeymoon. They were going to trade Carew anyway. He was one year away from free agency, and everybody knew Calvin wasn't going to pay him what he was worth.

Rodney was very moody, and he admitted it. He was always in a bad mood when he was going great at the plate. I got along with him, but boy, if you got on his bad side or did something to offend him, that was it.

Years later, I went out to Anaheim when his daughter Michelle was being treated for leukemia. I was at the hospital with him and Marilynn. Man, that was terrible. Just awful. She was their youngest kid, just 18 years old at the time. It ripped him apart when Michelle died in April 1996. The marriage came to an end after that too.

With guys like Oliva and Carew on the team, the baby boomers—and the next generation too—were spoiled on a damn good first decade of baseball here in Minnesota. Just a few years after reaching the World Series in 1965, the Twins put together more powerhouse teams in 1969 and '70, winning nearly 100 games both years. They just ran into tough Baltimore Orioles teams in the playoffs.

The on-field success built the team's popularity, and the Twins led the American League in total attendance during the '60s. They averaged 1.4 million per year. It was a great decade.

The following decade was not so great. There was no "Cheap Calvin" in the '60s; "Cheap Calvin" coincided with Carew's heyday in the '70s. For that generation of fans, Rodney was their man because he was the only thing they had. There are all kinds of 70-year-olds like me for whom Tony was their favorite player. And there are all kinds of 50-year-olds for whom Rodney was their franchise player.

I take great pleasure in knowing that I'm one of the few guys who can needle Rodney. After he recovered from his heart attack, I told him, "You and I are the same age. Too bad you didn't take care of yourself like me."

Sir Rodney is what I called him in print. He was one of a kind.

■ ■ ■

Gene Mauch was the most interesting baseball man I've ever covered, but Tom Kelly is the smartest baseball man I've ever been around.

TK came to the Twins in '83 as Billy Gardner's third base coach. The minor leaguers had spring training in Melbourne back then while the big leaguers were training in Orlando, so you couldn't walk across the field and say hello to them like you can at Fort Myers these days.

Kelly was the best third base coach I ever saw. He employed the same thing as a third base coach as he did with everything else: logic. He told me recently about how he had Paul Molitor coach some games at third base when he was the bench coach because "I never think a guy should coach third base for a manager who hasn't coached third base." That was his logic. Kelly took great pride in being a good third base coach.

He was very loyal to "Slick"—Billy Gardner, who is a top-five all-time goofball. All the coaches lived together at the Super 8 motel during the season. It was a blue-collar collection of guys, including the wonderful Rick Stelmaszek as a bullpen coach.

Ray Miller replaced Gardner as manager during the '85 season, and then the Twins fired Miller with 23 games left in '86. TK was named interim manager for the rest of the season. Andy MacPhail spent six weeks convincing team owner Carl Pohlad to give the job to TK. Carl had wanted somebody older.

I had gotten to know TK a little when he was a coach, and after he became the manager everybody in the media learned just how terrible he was with quotes. You didn't get sound bites from TK. You got explanations. He looked at you to make sure you understood, and if you didn't, you got the explanation again. He was a bit like Gene Mauch in that way—you had to wait to get your answer, and you didn't interrupt him because he was going to give you a detailed explanation eventually.

TK and I had one disagreement in my years covering him. I had quoted him saying something about Rick Aguilera that offended Aggie. TK came to me and said, "I'm not sure I said that the way you wrote it." It was hardly a blowup.

The rumor was always that Chris Clouser, briefly the Twins CEO in 2000, wanted to get rid of TK after the season. The team wasn't drawing any fans, and they wanted to get a stadium. They didn't know what to do. They were desperate.

Clouser concluded that it was time to get rid of Kelly. TK went to Pohlad and said, "I want to do this one more year." He's smart enough to know that Clouser was a meteor flying across the sky and wouldn't be around long.

TK stayed one more year as the Twins manager. Recently he told me a story I had never heard before. "In the middle of that season," he said, "I missed a play. I'm sure that had happened before, but this was the first time I noticed it. I was yelling for our guys to 'turn two,' and there were already two outs. That bothered me for a couple of weeks."

When it happened again a month later, Kelly started to wonder if he was slipping. And in his own mind, a detail guy like he was, he couldn't bear to be slipping.

He went to see Carl after that season. He said taking the steps from Pohlad's office was the longest walk he ever made, but he had it in his mind that he wasn't as sharp as he had been, and it was time to go.

The 2001 squad had produced the Twins' first winning season since '92 and finished in second place in the division. TK said he thought they might have won the division if shortstop Cristian

Guzmán hadn't gotten hurt at the All-Star Game. The Twins went on to win the division in four of the next five seasons with a roster that TK had done so much to develop.

Kelly's knowledge of baseball was second to none. He could see a guy and tell whether he could play or not. He took the rap for David Ortiz being dropped by the Twins and then going on to have a Hall of Fame career with Boston. Kelly just wanted Ortiz not to leap out and try to pull a pitch that was off the plate.

TK is an admirer of ballplayers who play the game right, and he was always looking to share his knowledge. Kelly wouldn't tell somebody to do something. It would be, "You know, you might want to try this with that guy." Molitor, whose baseball knowledge is off the charts, told me that when he became a manager, he wrote down 10 pages of notes he had gathered from conversations with Kelly.

When TK was managing Orlando in the AA Southern League and, before that, at single-A Visalia, he worked with many of the guys who would form the core of the '87 championship team—Kent Hrbek and Tim Laudner and Gary Gaetti and Randy Bush. He always said, "If you can play in the Southern League, you can play anywhere."

They were such professionals and so committed to playing the game right. Kelly really had a hard time with some guys later on who didn't share that same commitment.

There are so many guys who stand out from the Twins teams of the '80s. I loved Randy Bush. And Kent Hrbek. Herbie was something else.

I'll never forget Herbie's major league debut, in 1981, when he hit a game-winning home run in the 12th inning at Yankee Stadium. I was going to rewrite my afternoon column on the kid hitting the home run. I looked in the phone book and got the Hrbek home phone number. His mom, Tina, answered. We talked for a while, and then I asked if Kent's father, Ed, was there. She said, "Yeah, he's right here." He was slurring his words because he had ALS. I didn't know that. I had a line in the column, "Ed sounded like he was celebrating that home run," but I took it out for some reason. A rare moment of caution, and I'm glad I did, because I soon found out about his ALS.

Another great Hrbek moment came in '82, during the first year in the Metrodome. Herbie hit a grand slam against Kansas City, and his dad was sitting in front of the press box. Ed pushed himself up with some assistance and joined in the standing ovation.

■ ■ ■

I can't write this book without talking about Ron Davis. All-timer. The story goes that the day he was traded to the Cubs in August '86, the guys were so relieved to have RD gone that Kirby Puckett was running and down the aisle of the bus leading everyone in a rendition of "Jimmy Crack Corn," which was the song Davis always sang when he entered a game. It was as if they had been cured of something.

One of my top memories of RD was a save against the White Sox at Comiskey in June of 1985. RD was having his usual messy night, and the White Sox had the tying run on third base with two outs. Davis was facing the left-hand-hitting Harold Baines, a future Hall of Famer. He got two strikes, then threw a slider, and Baines swung and missed.

The Twins had won. Yet nobody in a Twins uniform moved for about five seconds. All the Twins were stunned that Harold struck out, as was Harold. Finally, RD thrust a tentative fist into the air, and the Twins started jumping around in celebration. All the while, Harold had a look on his face that said, *How did that happen?*

One more tale shows how bad it was for RD with the Twins. He told me this one himself during spring training. It had me howling. He was on the Twins winter caravan on a swing through South Dakota. Tony Oliva was on the trip too, and made them take a detour to a farmhouse in the middle of nowhere where his wife's aunt lived. The aunt was older and getting around slowly, but she was a huge Twins fan. The Twins group arrived at the house, and Tony started introducing the players. When he got to Ron Davis, the aunt rose quickly from her chair and took a step toward him with her cane. In the end, though, they became buddies, as Davis arranged tickets for Tony's aunt and her son to attend the 1985 All-Star Game at the Metrodome.

■ ■ ■

The greatest thing about covering baseball is the guys you meet and the stories you hear. On a random day at spring training, you might meet Ted Williams, and that leads to a fabulous tale.

In the early '80s the Red Sox had spring training in Winter Haven while the Twins were nearby in Orlando, so we used to be over there all the time for games. Around this time, the Twins were turning a guy named Dave Engle into a catcher. He was a good hitter who had mostly been playing outfield and DH.

I was sitting in the Red Sox dugout one morning before either team had taken batting practice. I was waiting for a scheduled interview with a player when Ted Williams walked into the dugout. He sat down five feet from me and said, "You a Minnesota guy?"

I said, "Yep."

He said, "How's Sid doing?"

I said, "Still scooping the world."

Then he said, "How's that Engle kid doing?"

I said, "He's a good hitter. They're trying to make him a catcher. Hell of a nice guy."

I was wondering how Ted Williams knew him.

As soon as I saw Engle pop into the Twins dugout, I went over and asked, "What's this deal with Ted Williams?"

Dave told me that his father grew up with Williams in San Diego. Engle's dad ran Williams's baseball camp in Lakeville, Massachusetts. They were best of friends.

Sometimes you get gifts presented to you in the story department.

6

LOVE OF FOOTBALL BEGAN WITH GOPHERS

Despite having occasional fun at the expense of long-suffering Go-
phers football fans, head coach P. J. Fleck, and the University of
Minnesota's football program in general, Reusse held deep devo-
tion to that team throughout his youth and early adult years. The
arrival of the Vikings and decline of the Gophers after a storied
history provided ample column fodder from the gridiron over the
decades.

■ ■ ■

My dad, Richard, loved Gophers football. He loved it so much that
on Saturday mornings he would put a piece of paper on a clipboard
and draw a football field on it. Then he would chart the Gophers'
play-by-play throughout the game, with straight lines for runs and
dashes for passes. I mean, he *loved* the Gophers.

In 1954, when Minnesota was good and Iowa was good, my dad
took me to the Gophers–Hawkeyes game at Memorial Stadium
on the University of Minnesota campus. I had just turned nine.
It was the biggest crowd ever to that point at Memorial Stadium:
65,000. There was an overflow crowd, and they let people stand
against the wall behind the end zone. Somehow Richard maneu-
vered it so that I was kneeling at the back line of the end zone with

< 67 >

binoculars hanging around my neck. That was the game where Gophers halfback Bob McNamara returned a kickoff for a touchdown. He ran into a mass of Iowa players and his own players around midfield and came out the other side and ran into the end zone.

The Gophers scored again late in the game, and it looked like they were going to win. The kickoff went to Earl Smith—one of Iowa's two great running backs, along with Eddie Vincent—and he ran it all the way back for an apparent touchdown. Suddenly, a huge cheer went up from the other end of the field. There was a penalty flag. The refs were bringing it back—no touchdown. I was kneeling in my spot at the edge of the end zone, and Smith was standing right above me. He responded to hearing that the touchdown was being called back with an audible profanity.

That was my first Gophers game. The Gophers won in dramatic fashion, and I learned a profanity from Earl Smith that has served me too well through the decades.

My second live Gophers game was in '59, when my brother was a student at the U. I came up and spent the weekend with him, and we watched the Gophers lose the season finale to Wisconsin. When we walked back to Michael's dorm after the game, we saw coach Murray Warmath hanging in effigy.

Every year was spent waiting for the Gophers football season to start. I remember riding my bike into town in 1957 to see if the college football preseason magazines had arrived. *Street & Smith* was the big one, but there were a few others. One of the magazines had Bobby Cox, the Gophers quarterback, on the cover. It was basically telling us that the Gophers were going to be national champions because we had a good season in '56.

They started off the '57 season with a 46–7 thumping of the University of Washington at Memorial Stadium. Cox was hurt for that game, which led to a memorable headline in the next day's sports section: "Gophers Defeat Washington with Cox Out." We grade-schoolers in Fulda got some giggles over that.

Laughter turned to tears three games later when the Gophers went to Illinois. We were 3–0 at that point, but the Illini found special motivation. The team brought Red Grange, the legendary Illinois superstar from the 1920s, to the locker room before the game to tell the players about a memorable Illini loss to Minnesota in 1924, and he asked for revenge.

Illinois destroyed us 34–13 that day in 1957. That game left me as depressed as I've ever been as a sports fan. I thought we were going to the Rose Bowl, but the Gophers ended the season with a 4–5 record. The next two seasons were even worse: 1–8 and 2–7. The power crowd from downtown Minneapolis wanted Warmath out.

Fortunately for Warmath, he had started to integrate the Gophers football program. He brought in Black players, primarily from Pennsylvania and North Carolina, and the team's fortunes started to turn. In 1959 sophomore Sandy Stephens was the starting quarterback. Tackle Bobby Bell was a freshman in '59 and not yet eligible for varsity competition, but he was a starter the following year.

The Gophers made it to the Rose Bowl in 1960. After winning their first six games, the No. 3 ranked Gophers beat No. 1 ranked Iowa at Memorial Stadium, which in my mind was the greatest game ever. They lost to Purdue the following week, and then they beat Wisconsin, moving back to the No. 1 ranking in the nation. The Associated Press voting took place at the end of the regular season in that era, and the Gophers were crowned national champions with an 8–1 record.

They lost to Washington 17–7 in the Rose Bowl on January 2. They played terribly that day and were beat by a fine quarterback, Bob Schloredt, who happened to be blind in one eye.

Stephens led the Gophers to the Rose Bowl again in '61, but they had some help to get there. The Pacific Coast Conference—a precursor to the Pac-10 and the Big Ten's regular Rose Bowl opponent since 1947—had disbanded following the 1958–59 season in the wake of a major scandal. This voided the Rose Bowl contract between the two conferences, which meant the no-repeat rule that had existed before was not in effect in '61, and the Gophers were eligible to play in the Rose Bowl again.

Also, the league stipulation that the conference champion represent the Big Ten in the Rose Bowl was off the table. The Ohio State Faculty Senate voted against allowing the Buckeyes to go to the Rose Bowl because they disliked coach Woody Hayes and didn't want to be known as just a football school. Not surprisingly, there were riots in Columbus over this decision.

The Gophers finished the regular season 6–1 in the conference and were the Big Ten runners-up, behind the 6–0 Buckeyes. The Rose Bowl called with an invitation and we said, *Hell yeah*. Then the Gophers went out and beat UCLA bad, 21–3.

That period was also the start of the international officiating conspiracy against the Gophers. Bobby Bell got an infamous roughing-the-passer penalty against Wisconsin quarterback Ron Vander Kelen in 1962. No Gophers player, coach, or fan believed Bell deserved that penalty, which came on a pass that was intercepted late in the game. I believe the official's name was Bob Jones. Sid Hartman was just a small part of the group that was bad-mouthing the officials for screwing over our Gophers.

As odd as it seems today, given the teams' relative popularity in Minnesota, there was much more excitement around Gophers football in the early '60s than there was around the arrival of the Vikings as a National Football League expansion team. In January '60 it was announced that Minnesota would be getting the league's 14th franchise in 1961.

Minnesota had been targeted as a cornerstone franchise for the new American Football League, which was preparing to start up with eight teams in 1960. Indeed, the inaugural AFL draft was held at the Pick-Nicollet Hotel in downtown Minneapolis in December of '59.

Charlie Johnson, who was the crotchety executive sports editor of the *Minneapolis Star* and *Tribune*, wrote an un-bylined commentary saying we didn't want an AFL team because we were a big-league town and should be part of the NFL.

Chicago Bears owner George Halas had promised the Minnesota group behind the AFL franchise that they would get an NFL team if they abandoned the new league. The NFL was terrified of the AFL driving up player costs, which it did.

Max Winter, representing the potential Minnesota franchise, was sitting in the lobby in Miami at the NFL meetings in January 1960. Pete Rozelle was elected the new commissioner at those meetings, and the NFL gave Dallas a team for the upcoming season and awarded Minnesota a team for 1961.

Truth is, we didn't really care about getting the Vikings because we had the Gophers going to the Rose Bowl.

As far as the Vikings were concerned, their first game in 1961 was phenomenal, with the rookie Fran Tarkenton at quarterback. They beat the Bears 37–13. But I was still much more interested in the Gophers. It took a long time for that to change. Never in the Norm Van Brocklin era, when he was head coach from 1961 to '66.

The Gophers' attendance started to slip later in the '60s, but I'm not sure that was because of the Vikings. The Vikings weren't a hard ticket to get during the Van Brocklin years. In '64 they had a good year and almost qualified for the Playoff Bowl, which was the runner-up game back them. Then they went backward in '65, and that's when Van Brocklin quit and came back the next day.

It was quite the competition in town between sportswriters Jim Klobuchar and Sid Hartman to see who could glorify Tarkenton the most. Klob had the advantage in that he would just make up quotes for him.

Things truly changed in terms of popularity for the two football teams at the end of the '60s. Van Brocklin left, and Vikings general manager Jim Finks, who had a background in the Canadian Football League, brought in Bud Grant from Winnipeg in '67. When Finks told his PR man, Bill McGrane, to pick up Grant at the airport, McGrane asked, "How will I know who he is?" Finks's response: "Just bring me the guy who looks like the town marshal."

The Vikings went 3–8–3 in Bud's first season. People were saying, "Tie one for Bud." In one game he had his team kick a field goal against the Rams when they were behind 32–0.

Question: Bud, why did you kick a field goal?

Bud: I didn't want us to get shut out.

In '68 the Vikings made the playoffs and Warmath had a decent team with the Gophers. Then in '69 the Gophers were ranked in the Top 20 to start the season. We had expectations. We had Jim Carter, the great fullback.

For the season opener, the Gophers went to Arizona State, which was in the Western Athletic Conference then. The Gophers had Jim Carter and power football and a proud defense. And they got 48 points scored on them.

It was 100 degrees that day. Carter ran for 200 yards, but it made no difference because as soon as Arizona State got the ball back, they had some very fast fellas zooming past the Gophers defense. It was like a track meet.

Jon Roe was there covering it for the Minneapolis paper. After the game, he said Warmath was sweating beyond belief. He had his shoes off and his pants rolled up and his feet in a bucket of ice water. Murray looked up and said, "Who scheduled this game?"

Then, eight days later, Vikings quarterback Joe Kapp threw seven touchdowns against the Baltimore Colts in a 52–14 victory. Met Stadium was full because people were optimistic about the team.

Right there, those eight days are what transformed the popularity of the two teams. This became a Vikings town and state. The Gophers fell off the radar. They finished 4–5–1. And Bud took the Vikings to the Super Bowl.

I didn't deal with the Vikings much in those years. I always kind of thought the media adulation was over the top. It was like they were infallible.

I did cover the Vikings' third Super Bowl, the one against the Pittsburgh Steelers in January '75 at Tulane Stadium. I had a seat in the press box between Jim Murray and Red Smith—two legends in the business. I was 24 years old, hungover to the teeth, and wearing an ugly sport coat. Red Smith was to my right. Jim Murray was on my left. I sat down and said, "Here we are, boys. Three of the greatest sportswriters that ever lived."

Smith gave a chuckle. Murray looked at me like I was insane, which I was.

That's the Super Bowl the Vikings should have won, by the way. Down 2–0 at halftime and they lost 16–6.

After the Vikings stunk out Tulane Stadium, my sidebars were kind of stern. As you can probably guess, I took the negative angle.

The following year, the St. Paul paper said they were sending me back to the Super Bowl. The Vikings were playing the Oakland Raiders at the Rose Bowl Stadium in Los Angeles. A week later, the editors said, "Uh, no, you're not going to the Super Bowl." The publisher of the *St. Paul Pioneer Press* and *Dispatch* at the time, Bernie Ridder, was also a part owner of the Vikings. Bernie wasn't terribly sensitive, but the editors were afraid that he was. They were afraid the Vikings were going to get their asses kicked, and I was going to rip them—and they were right.

After I started writing columns for the paper, I introduced the term "Horseshoe Harry" for Bud. At the *Dispatch* I could get away with anything. I wrote that Bud had a horseshoe where only his proctologist can find it—and it got in! That line wouldn't have a chance of seeing print 40 years later.

I didn't always believe in the reverence given to Bud. Often during my career, I had a hard time gaining full appreciation for people who are unique. They agitate me, but then I finally get to the point where I realize, *You know, there is only one of these. Get on the bandwagon.*

There was only one Bud, and I came to appreciate that. Now I admire him and admire his son Mike. But it took me a while.

The sports editor at the St. Paul paper had hired a new Vikings writer who shall go nameless, and three weeks into training camp, the editor decided he hated the way the guy wrote. The Twins were bad then, so he flipped that guy onto the Twins, and somebody else was going to take over the Vikings beat. In the meantime, they needed someone to go to Anaheim for an exhibition game. They got me on the Vikings team plane to go cover the game.

Bud was sitting in the seat in front of me. We had had only brief conversations before this moment. He turned around during the flight and talked to me for 45 minutes. Then—boom—that was it. Conversation over. He turned back around in his seat.

I had another observation that I wanted to make, so I tapped him on his shoulder. He didn't budge. I got my 45 minutes and that was it.

That reminds me of another Bud story I heard about. Mike Lynn, Vikings CEO at the time, had found his first corporate sponsor. The team brought out the executives and some of the big clients for this outfit for a gathering in Mankato during training camp on a Wednesday night after practice. They fed them and gave them drinks and had some of the players and coaches come and mingle. Bud was gracious and nice.

The next morning, one of these corporate guys was standing down at Gage Hall, where the Vikings stayed during training camp. This guy walked up to Bud with his hand out, all enthusiastic, like he's greeting an old friend. Bud looked at him and said, "We did that yesterday."

The lesson: Bud Grant had his boundaries, and you didn't want to cross them.

In the late '70s, Bud had a falling out with his star defensive tackle Alan Page and let him go. Page had gotten too skinny. He got down to 220 pounds from running so much. Bud was irate. I supported Alan in the whole feud, not that the *St. Paul Dispatch* had much sway.

When he was done playing, Alan went to work for Ed Garvey in the players union. Garvey was a great agitator. Just funnier than hell. He never won a war with the league, but he had a great way of annoying them.

One year the union reps were making their annual visit to Mankato for training camp, and Alan came with them. Garvey and Page were going to meet with the players sometime after lunch. Bud was leaving the cafeteria just as Garvey and Page were five feet from the door. Bud looked at Alan, and I got the impression that these guys had not talked in the five years since Bud let him go.

Bud said, "Well, look who's here."

It was 94 degrees and humid that day, but it suddenly felt 52 and frosty. I mean, it was unbelievable.

Bud and Alan shook hands, but there was no "Nice to see you" or anything. They nodded, and that was it. Two hard-headed individuals.

■ ■ ■

After the Vikings lost to the Kansas City Chiefs in the Super Bowl following the '69 season, my brother and I noticed how upset Vikings fans became and how strong was their belief in the team's infallibility. In later years, we'd watch the NFC title game, and then if the Vikings won, which they did three more times, we would go to a couple of bars in Prior Lake. We would start bad-mouthing the Vikings, saying they're going to get their butts kicked again. We'd end up getting points from people, and the bartenders would hold the bets for the Super Bowl. My brother and I probably made a couple of hundred bucks apiece in each of those next three Super Bowls. We agitated the Vikings fans into those bets. Michael could do that with the best of them.

Of course, the playoff game against the Cowboys to end the Vikings' 1975 run was a fantastic event. Longtime Vikings fans still love to gripe about the final play, when Dallas receiver Drew Pearson appeared to push off on cornerback Nate Wright to grab the game-winning Hail Mary touchdown pass from Roger Staubach, giving Dallas the 17–14 win. I was crowded into the Cowboys locker room after the game. The players were answering questions, and all of a sudden members of the Minnesota media began shouting that Pearson pushed off on the long winning pass and should have been penalized for pass interference.

Sid was screaming at referee Armen Terzian, who had a bandage on his head after getting nailed by a whiskey bottle thrown by a Vikings fan. Reporters used to be able to knock and just go in to talk to the referees. Sid burst in there and started yelling at Terzian, who looked like he'd been in a battle.

During the ensuing down years of the late '70s and early '80s, receiver Ahmad Rashad was one of the team's biggest stars. And he was one of the players I most liked to agitate. Ahmad had turned himself into quite the celebrity. In 1982 *Sports Illustrated* asked him to do a four-part diary about the season.

At the time, I was writing columns for the *St. Paul Dispatch*, which was not a widely circulated paper, especially on the west side of the river. I always said that I could write anything I wanted to because it would take three days for anybody to find out.

I didn't mind Ahmad, but I found him overly arrogant. In my columns, I would always sneak in a shot about him not going over the middle, that he only worked the sidelines. He came up to me during week two of the diary and said, "I saw what you wrote about me not going over the middle."

I said, "For god's sake, Ahmad. *Sports Illustrated* has six million readers. They're honoring you every week. You're the hero of American sports. What do you care about what's in the St. Paul paper?"

He was never hostile to me, never screaming obscenities. He was too smooth for that. But I was happy to see that he noticed what I had written. I don't know how he did. Somebody must have told him about it.

In one part of the diary he said he had been hit hard only three times in his life—which kind of supported my point that he didn't go over the middle. But anyway, during a game in Detroit, a defensive back named James Hunter came up and hit Ahmad in the middle of his back and broke a bone. The lead in my next day's column was, "Dear diary, make that four times."

We didn't know it then, but that was the end of Ahmad's playing career.

■ ■ ■

I've always had a lack of romanticism when it comes to the Vikings, but I developed a good relationship with Mike Lynn. Remarkable Mike. Lynn had the problem of the perpetual smirk. He couldn't get it off his face, so he always looked like he was up to something.

We wondered where this guy came from when he suddenly appeared at the Vikings–Steelers Super Bowl. Max Winter had run into him at NFL meetings when Lynn was trying to get a team for Memphis, where he ran a small business. Instead, he got hired by the Vikings.

Mike was a character. The guys who worked for him loved him. The players didn't, because he always fought them for every nickel, and he made some blunders, obviously. But the staff loved him. He treated them well. He'd always say, "You're my guy."

I got along with Mike for some reason. He's the only guy to win Turkey of the Year and call me on Thanksgiving morning and say, "It's about time."

He was smart that way. He could either fight you or schmooze you, so he would schmooze you. Then, of course, the trade for Herschel Walker in 1989 turned out to be a disaster.

Lynn is also the reason the Super Bowl came to Minnesota in 1992. First he got the NFL owners to vote that they were going to have another northern Super Bowl (the first since '82, when it was played at the Pontiac Silverdome in Michigan). Then he got them to agree on three finalist cities: Seattle, Detroit, and Minneapolis. He knew they weren't going back to Detroit. He put all his energy into getting enough votes for Minneapolis and Detroit in the first round to eliminate Seattle. He knew we could beat out Detroit. He didn't think we could beat Seattle. To get a Super Bowl played in that very mediocre stadium, the Metrodome, was a phenomenal accomplishment.

Remarkable Mike was always up to something, and a little revenge was fine with him too. After I had taken plenty of shots at him through the years, he called me up one day and said he had a column idea for me. I said I could use one because it was early summer and not much was going on. He said they were giving this kid a tryout. Really great story, he said. A long shot out of nowhere, but the coaches were pretty excited about him and thought maybe he could make the team as an offensive lineman.

I took the bait and talked to the kid. I never checked with the coaches. Turns out, they had never heard of the guy. He was marrying Lynn's daughter's best friend. Lynn's wedding gift to them was getting a column about the kid printed in the Minneapolis paper. I called Lynn and he said, "Boy, you took that one hook, line, and sinker. You should have checked a little more."

■ ■ ■

Even after the Vikings became the main attraction and the Gophers became more irrelevant, I continued to cover the college team. One of my great moments came when I was writing a sidebar for a Michigan game at Memorial Stadium in 1973. Michigan was kicking their tails. I was working the Michigan locker room for the postgame, and you had to walk through the stands to get there, so I left the press box with about five minutes to go in the game. I told the security guard I was with the media, and he opened the door to the Michigan locker room and let me in. I walked in and stood quietly in the back.

About 10 minutes later, the Michigan team came in. I was standing there trying to make my 250 pounds invisible. Michigan coach Bo Schembechler started telling his players what a horse-dung team they just beat. He was vilifying the Gophers in the most profane language. Then he said to an assistant, "Let 'em in." The other reporters came into the locker room, and I kind of popped out from behind Schembechler. He turned around and looked at me. He didn't say anything, but you could tell he was thinking, *Where the hell did this guy come from?* I got to hear vintage Bo. That was great.

In the '70s and early '80s, the Gophers had a long stretch where they would beat somebody good and then lose to a weak team like Indiana the next week. That's what happened for Cal Stoll in his best season as the Gophers head coach, 1977. They shut out No. 1 Michigan 16–0, and the next week they lost 34–22 at Indiana.

Cal was great in victory. I never gave him proper credit for being a pretty good guy. One of my favorite quotes of his came after the Michigan upset.

The Gophers had a really good defense. On one play, defensive tackle Steve Midboe was chasing Michigan quarterback Rick Leach. Leach was going left, right, left, right. He finally collapsed for a 20-yard loss. After the game, Stoll said, "He would have chased him all the way to Stub & Herb's."

Cal was a salesman, and the team needed it then. Attendance started going in the tank, and the Vikings kept going to the Super Bowl.

Even after their peak heyday was over, the Vikings were still Minnesota's top sports attraction in the early '80s, but the Gophers popped up when Lou Holtz arrived as coach in 1984. I started to needle him almost immediately because I just didn't like his rah-rah bull-slinging. I don't like the super hard sell from coaches.

All that being said, in Holtz's defense, he led an amazing turnaround for the team. The '83 Gophers were one of the worst teams in the history of college football. They beat Rice to open the season, and then they gave up 500 points in the next 10 games and finished 1–10.

The Gophers were trying to hire Les Steckel to replace Smokey Joe Salem as head coach, but then the Vikings hired Steckel after Grant quit.

So the Gophers hired Lou—who had good success at Arkansas and North Carolina State—and you know Minnesota: we couldn't believe that he came here. We just gobbled it up. Sid was head over heels for him because Sid knew him from when Lou was a grad assistant at Iowa. I didn't like the whole shtick. It was obvious to me that he was full of baloney. I started calling him "The Music Man."

While I was working at the St. Paul paper, we had a Holtz lookalike contest. I went in on Sunday to write about it. You could get away with stuff on Sunday because no editors or bosses were there. An artist at the paper was a buddy of mine and would do anything I asked. I went up to the newsroom library and got a picture of the actor Robert Preston from *The Music Man* film. We also cut out a picture of a mini Gophers logo. We put the little Gopher on Preston's hat. The joke didn't get revealed until the column jumped inside the sports section. I wrote that I found the perfect candidate for a Holtz look-alike. You jumped inside and there was Robert Preston with a Gopher on his hat.

Next day, I got a call at home from the editor, Deborah Howell. Boy, was she mad. She said, "Come in here! I want to talk to you." I went in and she said, "We don't alter photos!"

That Christmas, in the morning paper we had Santa and his reindeer across the top of the front page. A couple of days later I went into the office and threw the paper down on Deborah's desk and said, "I thought we didn't alter pictures around here. Did you really see Santa's sleigh?!"

Holtz left Minnesota after two seasons to coach at Notre Dame. Shortly after Holtz left, Sid went to pick up his son, Chad, from the airport on his arrival from three months away at Arizona State. Chad was expecting a warm greeting. Instead, Sid was so distraught over Holtz's departure, he barely said hello.

Holtz came back to Minnesota in February 1986 to talk to the St. Paul Notre Dame Club. This was just a few months after he announced he was leaving. It was a packed house. I went to the event, and he actually talked to me, despite all the shots I had taken at him. But I said to myself, *He was born to coach Notre Dame.* I also went to his first game at Notre Dame, which was against Michigan. I went to the Friday night pep rally and thought, *Yup. He's home.*

Although the Gophers didn't do much under Holtz, Mike Lynn was in a panic when Lou was here because of all the media attention he got. That's when Lynn got Bud to come back to coach the Vikings. In '84 the Vikings went 3–13 and the Gophers were the bigger draw. The whole town was talking about the Gophers, and nobody was talking about the Vikings—until Lynn brought Bud back. I think if Lou had stayed, it would have been a long time before the Vikings regained their uncontested popularity.

■ ■ ■

Bud was back as Vikings coach for only one season ('85), and then Jerry Burns was the head coach from 1986 to '91. It was fun getting to know Burnsie. We didn't have much access to him when he was the Vikings' offensive coordinator from 1968 to '85. Bud didn't want his assistants being quoted in the media.

A lot of players during Burnsie's tenure were not thrilled when it came to dealing with the press. Scott Studwell was the worst if he didn't think you were properly on board with the team.

Studwell was a great linebacker for the Vikings from 1977 to '90, and he was hired by Jerry Reichow as a scout after his playing career was over. Reichow—one of the great old-timers who spent nearly 60 years with the Vikings organization in a variety of roles, including as a player in 1961–64—was the director of player personnel when Burnsie was the coach. Reichow had enormous admiration for Studwell's work ethic and judgment on players. As Studwell rose through the ranks in the front office, Reichow's full endorsement was always there.

In 1994 I was at Vikings practice in Mankato a few days after Sid introduced Bud Grant at Canton for his induction in the Pro Football Hall of Fame. Studwell was standing close to the field, actually watching what was going on, rather than standing there b.s.-ing like us sportswriters.

I walked over and said, "Scott, when you get into Canton, I just want you to know that I'm available to introduce you, as Sid did for Bud." Studwell said something like, "In the unlikely event I get there, I'll keep that offer in mind."

Burnsie's Vikings made the most astounding playoff run in franchise history after the 1987 strike-interrupted season. That team was 0–3 with replacement players and 8–7 overall, losing its last two games with the regular players. Minnesota needed an upset by Dallas over St. Louis on the last Sunday to back into the NFC playoffs.

My column on the morning of the first playoff game against the New Orleans Saints was filled with ridicule over the very idea that Burnsie's "Back Door Gang," as I called them, had any worthiness to be involved in the NFC playoffs. I had to eat a lot of newsprint after the Vikings trounced the Saints, 44–10. Still, I was delighted for quarterback Wade Wilson, a terrific guy known to teammates as "Whiskey." I think that was mostly because he wasn't as enthusiastic about consuming it as were Tommy Kramer and numerous other teammates.

Old St. Paulites still mention to me the "Purple Triangle" column of the mid-1980s. The Vikings had accumulated 13 DUI stops in 18 months, mostly in the Eden Prairie–Bloomington area. Again on a Sunday when no editors were around to kill the story, I got my artist pal to put little purple helmets on a map in roughly the areas where the stops had taken place. The column included advice to avoid driving in those areas between 6:00 PM Thursday and Monday morning. There was a guide to each of the DUI locations, with little helmets showing the player's number on them.

You can imagine how that went over with the Vikings.

Then Denny Green came to town in '92. The great myth of Denny is that he was always in a feud with the local media. That's not true. For three years the "new sheriff in town" mantra wasn't a joke. People used it a lot, but he was good. The Vikings were going downhill, and he redid the team. The first time he got ripped by the media was after the Vikings lost to the Chicago Bears in the '94 wild card playoff game, because that made him 0–3 in the playoffs. He didn't take it too well.

A month later, Selena Roberts and Curt Brown, the two beat writers for the *Star Tribune*, came out with an investigative report on sexual harassment within the Vikings coaching staff. That's when the relationship between Green and much of the local media went way south.

I ripped Denny a few times for various things, but mostly I would have fun with him because I could see how thin-skinned he was. I don't think I ever denied that he was a good offensive coach, especially considering the dubious quality of many of the quarterbacks who came through during those years.

In '97, as his frustration with the media continued to bubble over, Green made his crazy cabal accusation before a playoff game against the New York Giants. The Vikings had lost in the first round of the playoffs the previous year, so Green was 0–4 in the playoffs at that point. He knew he would get fired if he lost to the Giants. Before the game he told ESPN reporter Andrea Kremer that a cabal of three columnists in town got together with a Vikings official and conspired to run him out of town. He never named who was in the cabal. Just three guys. The assumption was the trio he was talking about was *Star Tribune* columnist Dan Barreiro, the *Pioneer Press*'s Tom Powers, and me.

I wrote a column a couple of days later saying how terrible it was that Denny said those things about Barreiro, Powers, and Bob Sansevere (also from the *Pioneer Press*), and that they were all really nice guys. At the end, I facetiously added that an editor asked if I was sure that I had the right three guys. I wrote that it had to be because I didn't think he would put Sid in that group.

But I have to admit, it would have gotten ugly if the Vikings had made the Super Bowl like they should have after the '98 regular season. "Poor, tortured Denny overcomes bias and takes Vikings to Super Bowl" would have been the story line.

That season changed the public's whole mindset about the Vikings, and that level of enthusiasm still exists today. It created a new generation of people interested in the team. My generation was cynical as hell about them because we went through the four Super Bowl losses. Now if you say bad things about the Vikings, the under-50 crowd gets mad at you. They get very defensive.

It's amazing the impact that season had, but that final game could be the worst loss in franchise history. I remember my friend Mark Whicker coming up to me before the game saying that the vibe felt like when the San Diego Chargers upset heavily favored Pittsburgh in the 1994 AFC Championship Game because nobody was considering the possibility that the Vikings could lose, which is how everyone felt about the Steelers a few years earlier.

And then Bob Ryan from the *Boston Globe* said, "You know what's bad karma? Gary Anderson having not missed a kick all year."

Still, Vikings fans never imagined that the bad karma would come to fruition. Even five seconds after Anderson missed the field goal to lose that NFC Championship Game to the Falcons, the crowd was still going nuts with joy because the idea that he actually missed didn't occur to anybody. But then reality hit.

One of the most tragic scenes I've seen in Minnesota sports happened while I was walking back to the office to write my column, about an hour and 15 minutes after the game. The *Star Tribune* building was across from the Metrodome back then. There was a parking lot between the Dome and the offices. The ground was slushy, and there were about 150 Vikings window flags lying on the ground in that lot. People just ripped them off their cars. They were beside themselves.

The *Star Tribune*'s Brian Peterson took a photo of three dejected female fans in the stands after the loss. I call it the "Weeping Blondes" photo, and I think it's the best photo ever taken. I have it in my garage. Every day when I get in the car, I give them a wink.

You know what: as shocking as the loss was, Atlanta was a good team. They went 14–2 that year. They played fantastic. Falcons quarterback Chris Chandler handled the Metrodome crowd magnificently. The Vikings were better than them and should have won the game, but it wasn't like they were playing a team of chumps.

Yeah, it was the worst Vikings loss ever, there's no doubt about it. Worse even than the 41–doughnut loss of two years later.

I was amazed at the free pass Vikings fans gave Randy Moss for his no-show performance in that 41–0 loss to the Giants in the NFC Championship Game. It was 14–0 barely two minutes into the game, and after a couple of early Vikings drives flamed out, Moss quit on his team. He gave a half-hearted effort on most of his routes.

The game was being played in New York, and the Vikings were still favored to win by two points, which told you how unimpressed people were with the Giants as a team. All week leading up to the game, the "inside word," as Sid would tell us, was that the optimism held by Green and his staff was enormous. In the end, the overconfident Vikings staff was badly outcoached by the Giants' crew of head coach Jim Fassel, defensive coordinator John Fox, and offensive coordinator Sean Payton in the greatest one-day coaching mismatch I've witnessed in an important game.

By the middle of the second quarter, the Minnesota media corps was in a fierce contest to see who could come up with the best one-liners of ridicule. Eventually, even the *Tribune*'s Kevin Seifert—the best overall beat writer I've had the privilege to work with, and a guy who is also very dignified—couldn't resist. He noticed the Vikings defensive backs dashing out on the slightest pump fake by Giants quarterback Kerry Collins, and he said they looked like dogs on a beach being duped by their owner with fake Frisbee tosses.

Several Vikings staff members were in the row behind us in the press box, including team executive Rob Brzezinski. I ran into him in the men's room at halftime, and he reviewed my participation in the first-half quips in critical fashion. I don't recall my exact reply, but it was suggested that Brzezinski reserve his anger for the gentlemen involved in game preparation who were trailing 34–0 at that moment.

Marty York, a Toronto sportswriter noted for odd scoops, came up with the story that the Giants might have been intercepting the Vikings offensive communications from the coaches' booth upstairs. KFAN's primary Vikings' apologists went all in on that for a couple of days, but then the theory died out. Instead, we live with Moss's one great contribution on that outrageous afternoon in New Jersey: "41-doughnut."

7

PERSONALITIES THAT STAND THE TEST OF TIME

Reusse has interviewed countless subjects throughout his sports-writing career, enough to fill a phone book. To him, that's one of the best parts of the job, especially when those interactions involve colorful personalities.

This chapter belongs to the select few who deserve their own category. They had big personalities. They were true characters and legends in every sense.

■ ■ ■

Jerry Burns was the definition of an all-timer.

Burnsie loved football players. *Loved them.* His admiration for them ran deep, especially for the great, hard-nosed football players. He loved 'em all, the ones who competed for him and tried all the time. Even when they screwed up, he expressed his love for his players. As Burnsie said about fullback Alfred Anderson during his infamous postgame rant in '89: "It was a dumb play by Anderson. I love Anderson. But it was a dumb fucking play."

That rant, of course, became legendary. During a postgame press conference, he went on an extended, profanity-filled diatribe defending his offensive coordinator, Bob Schnelker—and this was after a game the Vikings *won.* I was proud to participate

< 87 >

when writer Dom Cosentino from the website Deadspin called me in 2018 and said he had run across the outburst and felt it was horribly underrated in the realm of coaching rants. Cosentino did a celebratory piece that gained considerable attention, back when Deadspin still was a hot outlet for being irreverent.

One of Burnsie's sons-in-law told me it was a rite of passage in the family that when one of their kids turns 15, they play the Schnelker rant for them and say, "This is Grandpa."

Only a few of us got to witness another classic Burnsie rant. In December 1987 the Vikings had lost the regular-season finale to Washington in a Saturday evening game, and it appeared that a very talented Vikings team was going to miss the playoffs. They were 8–7 officially, but the true Vikings team was 8–4, because three of the losses came with the replacement players who were part of the NFL's strike-breaking efforts.

A handful of sportswriters were having an interview session with Burnsie on Sunday morning after the Washington loss in a tiny media workroom adjacent to the locker room at Winter Park. There were five spots in that workroom if you squeezed in, and also a bathroom behind what wasn't a soundproof door. When it got too cold to interview players out on the practice field, you would try to get them to come in there for an interview. There was nothing quite as smooth as having a one-on-one with quote machine Jesse Solomon while another sportswriter used the commode in strenuous fashion five feet away, behind that thin door.

On that Sunday in '87, the Vikings needed St. Louis to lose to a bad Dallas team in order to reach the playoffs. Burnsie was depressed and being prodded to rip his team. Bob Sansevere, a fine agitator, suggested that the team was lacking in "killer instinct." What followed was a Burnsie rant deriding Sansevere's suggestion—as well as the rest of us who were ripping his team. No tape recordings exist of that one, so only a few of us are blessed with a proper appreciation of the "killer instinct" rant, which stands as 1B to the 1A of Schnelker on Burnsie's all-time list.

And he was a big winner after that one too. Dallas upset St. Louis. The Vikings went to New Orleans for the first playoff game. The city was nuts for the Saints, and Anthony Carter and the Vikings blew them out, 44–10.

They then went to San Francisco and manhandled the 49ers in the first half to the point that Joe Montana was booed off the field and replaced by Steve Young. Carter, with Wade Wilson on the trigger, was outstanding again.

They went to Washington for the NFC title game and lost a close one at the end as RFK Stadium was rocking madly. Vikings running back Darrin Nelson has been bad-mouthed for dropping a pass at the goal line in that game, but it was more a tremendous play by Washington's Darrell Green, an all-time great cornerback.

The Vikings went from no "killer instinct" to what came close to being a spectacular run to the Super Bowl: a blowout of an excellent Saints team, a beatdown of a dynastic 49ers team, and a near-win over a Joe Gibbs Washington team—all on the road.

Burnsie's hobby was golf. One time he got a hole in one. I called him up to do a little piece on his ace. All he did was bitch about making a six on the next par three. "Grrrr, I made a triple bogey. That hole in one was lucky. That six was the real me. This damn game."

He was something else.

■ ■ ■

My three all-time hockey guys are lumped together as a triumvirate: Glen Sonmor, Lou Nanne, and Herb Brooks.

I did not get to know Sonmor very well when he was coaching the Gophers from 1966 to '71. He led them to a Western Collegiate Hockey Association playoff championship in '71 and then got offered a job as general manager and coach of the new Minnesota Fighting Saints franchise in the World Hockey Association. The Gophers didn't pay coaches much money back then, so he took the job.

When I look back on my career, I regret that I basically ignored the Fighting Saints. The stories of their tenuous financial situation and the characters they had working there and Sonmor running the hockey operation—the whole thing was something else. I didn't become a columnist until '79, by which time the Saints were gone. But if I had been a columnist during their run in St. Paul, I would have had riches in stories. I mean *riches.*

Two guys named Gary Davidson and Dennis Murphy had started the American Basketball Association as an alternative league to the NBA in 1967, and they wanted to do something similar in hockey, so they started this World Hockey Association. And the upstart league signed some big names away from the NHL. The Winnipeg Jets signed Bobby Hull. The Houston Aeros signed Gordie Howe. The Saints' big guy was Mike "Shakey" Walton, whom they signed away from Boston. They also had Dave Keon, a future Hall of Famer, from the Toronto Maple Leafs.

The Fighting Saints played at the old St. Paul Auditorium when they first started. The team was being promoted heavily in the St. Paul paper by Don Riley and Charley Hallman. The North Stars had hit on hard times around then; after a honeymoon period of four or five years, they went into decline, and the owner started to trade talent away.

Sonmor, like me and several sportswriters at the St. Paul paper, had a drinking problem. Glen dried out the last time in '83 or '84 and spent the rest of his life working hard for AA, going to meetings and making visits to people to help get them sober. He was really hard-core in sobriety. Me, I just quit drinking.

I knew him well during our mutual drinking days. One night I was at the office trying to get the paper out, and it was snowing like hell. This had to be 1972. We made our usual mad dash across the street to Luigi's at 12:50 AM before closing time. When we got there we found a guy facedown in the snow, his outstretched arm reaching toward the door. We flipped him over and it was Glen.

We picked him up, brushed the snow off him, and brought him inside for a hot brandy. Then we took him for breakfast at 2:30 in the morning. He sobered up enough to tell us what a bunch of jerks we were for not giving the Fighting Saints more publicity. Sonmor was just one of the great story lines and characters from that team.

One example: They would distribute checks to the players on payday, and then it would be a mad sprint to the bank. The players would all rush out of the building and run to the bank. They wanted to have one of the checks that actually cleared. If you were slow, you had no chance.

Sonmor used to answer the phone at the office: "Minnesota Folding Saints, can I help you?"

One time, the players were refusing to make a road trip unless they got paid. The team was always broke, but owner Wayne Belisle and Sonmor had some connection at the Western Bank who kept bailing them out. Sonmor and Belisle went to the bank and got $25,000 cash, basically in a cigar box, and drove to meet the team at the airport, counting out the money. Sonmor was divvying up the dollars he could give to each player that would entice them to get on the plane.

As a coach, Sonmor loved fights. He had a few in his life too, even with the glass eye. He had lost his eye after getting hit by a puck on a slapshot during his playing days. There is a famous story about Glen from when he was coaching the Gophers. This was back in the days when you could have a riot on the ice and nobody would get thrown out of the game.

During the 1969–70 season, the Gophers were playing in Duluth. Mike Antonovich, Glen's all-time favorite player, was checked hard and was hanging over the top of the boards. A Duluth fan who had been heckling Sonmor all game reached out and grabbed Antonovich's stick and wouldn't let go. Glen stormed into the crowd and started throwing punches, whaling on the heckler. Somebody ripped off Glen's shirt. They didn't get his tie, but they ripped off his shirt. Glen went back to the bench, and the game started again. He was standing there with his tie hanging down the middle of his bare, hairy chest, and he was just grinning.

The original Fighting Saints franchise folded in 1976, and then the Cleveland team moved to St. Paul and became the New

Fighting Saints. After that team also folded, Sonmor became the coach and general manager of the Birmingham Bulls, who had entered the league in '76. It was a marriage made in heaven: Bear Bryant country, where people didn't know anything about hockey, and Sonmor was the coach.

Sonmor's Bulls set a professional hockey record for the most team penalty minutes. They had Steve Durbano, who was insane; Frank Beaton, a forward who fought everybody; Gilles Bilodeau, who was crazy; and Dave Hanson, who was in the movie *Slap Shot*.

Glen proudly displayed on his office wall a sports cartoon from the *Cincinnati Enquirer* of "Glen's Goons." The cartoon had him leading those four goons in with a chain, and there's blood coming off their fingers. That was Sonmor's office art.

After two years with the Bulls, Sonmor was hired to coach the North Stars. I was not Mr. Hockey and never have been. But I would go to games and go downstairs after the game ended around 9:45 PM. I'd already have an early column written. Then Glen would start talking, and next thing I know it's 11 o'clock and I'm hauling it back upstairs to start rewriting because I've been listening to him telling stories that are just hysterical.

Before Sonmor became the coach, the North Stars had never won in Boston. It drove Glen crazy to have a team that was perceived as not being tough enough to stand up to the Bruins. He got his players whipped up in a frenzy for that infamous Bruins–North Stars game in February 1981 where the fighting started as soon as the puck dropped and the teams finished with 400-something penalty minutes, setting the NHL record. Sonmor's tactic must have worked, because the North Stars went on to win a playoff series against the Bruins that year, taking the first two games in Boston, which seemed incomprehensible back then.

Later in life, Sonmor was going to live in Toronto with his sister, and I went to the send-off party. There must have been a hundred old hockey players there. Half Gophers, half North Stars. You could have written a book out of the stories flying that night about Sonmor.

The old hockey guys are the best storytellers. And Sonmor was numero uno. Well, maybe a tie between him and Tom Reid.

■ ■ ■

Lou Nanne came down from the Soo—Sault Ste. Marie—to play for the Gophers in 1960. Louie was a really good player. When he was 21, he started playing for the Rochester Mustangs in the original US Hockey League, and then he signed with the North Stars in 1967.

Here is all you need to know about Louie: He went from playing for the North Stars to being their general manager/coach. The North Stars ownership was having financial trouble, and they gave the job to Louie. They took him off the ice and made him the general manager/coach.

Nanne is the man who convinced the NHL that it was a reasonable idea to merge two teams and let one of them keep the best players. The North Stars were for sale in Minnesota. The Barons were dying in Cleveland. Somehow, Louie got to keep the best players from the Cleveland roster, and because the North Stars were the worst team in the league, they also let him keep the No. 1 draft pick, which was Bobby Smith. It's unbelievable how he pulled off that scam.

After he left the North Stars in 1988, he went into the investment business. I once told him about a friend of mine who had just sold his company for $42 million. I told Louie that he could probably get $2 million out of him. Louie said, "I don't want the two. I want the forty."

I named him "Turkey of the Year" once, and that strained our relationship briefly. He is the godfather of hockey here in Minnesota, that's for sure.

Herbie Brooks was a character too, and I liked to agitate him. When he coached the United States to the Olympic gold medal in 1980, everybody was going insane. I wrote, "Boy, it's amazing what you can do when you have a hot goalie," and stuff like that.

At the '84 Olympics, the US team tied lowly Norway in the preliminary round. I called up the Norwegian consulate and asked, "How do you say, 'Do you believe in miracles?' in Norwegian?"

The woman took a few minutes and spelled it out for me in Norwegian. That was the lede to my column. That night I ran into Herbie at a North Stars game. He said, "You really think you're funny, don't you?"

I said, "Come on, Herbie. That was pretty funny."

He did give me one of the great compliments of all time. He heard I had gone into alcohol treatment. According to my buddy Gregg Wong, who was tight with Brooks, Herbie called him and said, "I'm tired of getting libeled by that talented alcoholic."

I said to myself, *There's no denying the second part of that description. As for the talented part—hey, thanks, Herbie.*

■ ■ ■

When I was hired at the *St. Cloud Times* in May 1966, St. John's University was coming off its second national football title (the first was in '63). The school's athletic banquet was a week after I started at the paper, and they were celebrating the national title.

We ended up at John Gagliardi's house that night, which is when I first met him. Even though I didn't really cover him or St. John's football during my two and a half years in St. Cloud, I got to know him and found out what a character he was.

Once I became a columnist at the St. Paul paper in '79, I learned that if it was springtime or late summer and you really needed a column, just get in your car and drive up to Collegeville and see John. He always had some story to tell you.

Gags was innovative and willing to adapt. The Johnnies had a power running offense when they won the two national titles in '63 and '65. By 1976 the triple veer running attack was very popular in college football. Always the innovator, Gagliardi upped that to the quadruple veer with quarterback Jeff Norman, and the Johnnies defeated Towson State for a third national title. Later on,

John's teams were throwing the ball all over the place. Late '80s, '90s, they had great quarterbacks. John got into the idea that it's a lot easier to complete an eight-yard pass than to run for eight yards against good teams.

Gagliardi suffered more from defeat than anybody I've ever been around. His suffering was off the charts. He was an absolute wreck. He could barely speak.

One example of this was in the early '90s. He had a really good team, with a quarterback named Pat Mayew and a tremendous defensive tackle named Steve O'Toole. They were playing at Dayton—this was before Dayton moved out of Division III—and the Flyers were a powerhouse and played in this big, old, dank stadium.

John's team lost only 19–7, but they had 10 turnovers. Ten!

I headed down to the locker room after the debacle was over. John was in this huge empty space outside the locker room, sitting on a folding chair by himself with his head down. He just mumbled when I asked him questions.

Four or five seniors came out of the locker room to talk to John. He was inconsolable. He had his head down, and he said, "Ah, well, I'm replaceable. All the players are replaceable. We're all replaceable."

He looked up and saw O'Toole, his great senior tackle, walking out of the locker room, and John said, "Except him. He's not replaceable."

John was known for spending endless hours looking at game tape. He was an expert on it and an expert at splicing film in earlier years. Back in the day when teams had to exchange film before they played, the story was that John would send the opponent film that was, shall we say, missing some action. There would be a play and you'd see the quarterback rolling right and then you'd see a back running into the end zone. You don't know who blocked whom, who did what. If there was a play that John didn't want his upcoming opponent to see, he would edit it out.

His film sessions with his players were legendary because if a player screwed up, he would run the play and run it back and run it again. But the players all loved him because he was grandpa goof. All the players called him John. He wouldn't let them call him "Coach."

He coached hockey at St. John's for a while too, but he hated the cold. The school had an outdoor rink that was next to "Rat Hall," the basketball gym. He'd sit in a room up in Rat Hall with the window open a crack and coach practice from there. He didn't want to be outside freezing to death.

John also was a nationally renowned speaker at banquets. Various groups would bring him in to give speeches, and he was hilarious. His famous quote was "When the monks at St. John's told me they took a vow of poverty, I didn't know that included the coaches."

John was low-key and modest. I was there when he was winning the league every year and really had it going. I asked him, "John, what's your record since the last 15 years?"

He said, "Ah, geez, I don't know."

Then he started shuffling around his office like the absent-minded professor. He reached in a drawer and grabbed a sheet of paper that showed he had a better record than every other team in the country in that time frame. Man, I just loved the guy.

The referees hated him. Even if a guy had been refereeing in the league for 20 years, John would say, "Hey, you, come here. What's your name? I've got to write it down."

John apparently had a tape with plays that showed St. John's getting robbed by the officials. He would keep it year after year and add new stuff to it. And on Christmas Eve, his family would watch it as part of the holiday celebration.

Look at that clip! That should've been a clip. That wasn't a touchdown!

As I always say, there's nothing better than unique.

8

◆

FINDING HOOPS HEAVEN

Want to experience Reusse's nirvana? That would be an important Big Ten basketball game on a Saturday afternoon in late February with Bill Musselman or Clem Haskins prowling the sideline of the elevated court at Williams Arena.

Recently, Gophers basketball has lost its high standing in the sports market, and the evolution of the game has changed the way this crusty old sportswriter views the sport.

■ ■ ■

When I was a kid, high school basketball was a phenomenon in small-town Minnesota. You played football, but it didn't really lead to anything; there was no state tournament.

High school basketball in the winter was the thing. The farmers were active in the fall when the football season was going on. But in the winter, the whole town had their eyes on the basketball season. If you were looking for something to do, you'd go to the local gym to watch the basketball team.

In the '50s, before all the mergers, we probably had 200 more high schools than we have now. All these small-town teams were your rivals back then. Glencoe is now merged with Silver Lake, but they used to be big rivals.

I came from District 8, down in the southwest corner of the

< 97 >

state. About 30 miles west of Fulda, Edgerton was a small, raga-muffin town. It had about 900 people in 1960.

Edgerton made it to the district final in '59. Then in 1960 Edgerton was unbeaten heading into the last game of the season, but they had played the little towns up to that point. Luverne scheduled Edgerton for that final game. And Luverne played in the Southwest Conference, which included Marshall and Worthington and Windom and Slayton—bigger towns.

My buddies and I drove over from Fulda to Luverne for the game against Edgerton. It was standing room only in the gym, and we were standing up against a wall. They showed the game on closed-circuit TV next door in the cafeteria.

Luverne got off to something like a 10–0 lead. We were thinking, *Yeah, we knew these farm kids were frauds.*

Richie Olson, who was in his first year as the coach of Edgerton, called time-out following the slow start. He gave his players a pep talk, and they came out of the time-out and started making every shot. I thought, *Holy Christ. Look at this.* They were making shots from all over the place.

Starters Darrell Kreun, Leroy Graphenteen, Dean Veenhof, and Dean Verdoes made all-state from Edgerton. And you're not a real Edgerton savant if you don't remember the fifth starter: Bob Wiarda.

They beat Luverne and went on to win District 8 and the regional. Now the whole state was excited, because we loved it when a small school made it to the state tournament.

Edgerton played Chisholm in the first round of the state tournament. They outshot Chisholm and beat them in front of more than 18,000 in Williams Arena.

The second night they played Richfield, a suburban power that had the great Bill Davis. The refs ruined that game for both teams, calling fouls on everything. Both teams were in terrible foul trouble. Neither team got a fair shake, but Edgerton survived to win.

The next night, a Saturday, Edgerton was set to play Austin in the state championship game. Austin was a powerhouse, and they had a fantastic coach named Ove Berven. The legend was, if you had a really good basketball player in southeastern Minnesota, there was a fair chance Dad could get a job as a foreman at Hormel so the family would move to Austin.

When Austin came up the stairs onto the court at Williams Arena, most of the crowd of more than 19,000 booed lustily simply because Austin had the temerity to show up to play Edgerton.

Edgerton won the game 72–61. They beat Austin fair and square. They just made their shots. It topped off a perfect 27–0 season for the Flying Dutchmen.

The state went crazy when Edgerton won. The team had to wait until Monday for the reception back home because nobody did anything in Edgerton on Sundays. The team arrived home on Monday, and the people of southwest Minnesota showed up en masse. My father got in the parade by putting a red light on top of his station wagon and calling it an ambulance.

After the "big city" schools of Duluth Central and St. Louis Park won the state titles in 1961 and '62, Marshall won in '63 and then Luverne won in '64. So we had three state single-class champions within a 50-mile radius in southwestern Minnesota in a five-year span. Since switching to the multi-class format in 1971, the state basketball tournament can never recapture the magic of the single-class days.

■ ■ ■

Aside from the high school tournament, I was a big fan of Gophers basketball back then. I remember watching the Iowa–Minnesota game in 1955 on our grainy television. Minnesota had two great players in Dick Garmaker and Chuck Mencel. Iowa beat us in a heartbreaker, 72–70. Iowa was a tough team, and they went on to win the Big Ten that year.

Coach Johnny Kundla finally integrated the Gophers in the early '60s. He brought in Archie Clark, Lou Hudson, and Don Yates. Those three were outstanding. Hudson broke his wrist during his senior year (1965–66) and had to play left-handed. Lou was probably the all-time best Gophers basketball player.

The Gophers were a decent team around that time, but it wasn't like they captured the town for more than about 48 hours. And then Bill Musselman came in as coach and turned that team and its fan base around.

In '71 the U hired Cal Luther from Murray State to be the Gophers head basketball coach. He got here and saw Williams Arena and went right back to Murray State. He thought it was such a dump. He didn't think it was possible to win here. So the U hired the 33-year-old guy from Ashland University instead.

Musselman came in and broke out a Globetrotter-like pregame show. He had his players do fancy ball-handling routines and passing drills to the tune of "Sweet Georgia Brown," much like the old Globetrotters act. He had a player named "Crazy George" Schauer who could spin a ball on his finger, toss it over his head, and catch it behind his back. Another player, Mike Monson, rode a unicycle while juggling three balls. It was quite the production. The crowd went nuts every time. Fans started coming to games early just to see the warm-up routine.

Musselman walked into a basketball vacuum, and by the time the Gophers played Indiana in the Big Ten opener, the games were being broadcast on closed-circuit TV at the hockey arena next door because Williams Arena was so full.

That Indiana game was something else. The Gophers beat them 52–51. Sophomore forward Jim Brewer blocked a shot at the buzzer, and Indiana's Bobby Knight chased the officials off the court because they didn't call a foul.

The Gophers took over the city. They were the No. 2 attraction in town after the Vikings because the Twins had fallen into decline.

Musselman was great, in a wired-up, zany way. I followed him all over the country to write stories on him. I had a great relationship with him, but you had to realize that he was screwy. He never did anything half-heartedly.

The fight with Ohio State in 1972 ruined his reputation as a college coach. That made the NCAA say, "We've got to look at what's going on at Minnesota."

Center Ron Behagen had been a great player at Southern Idaho Junior College. The speculation was that the other Big Ten coaches had an unofficial agreement not to recruit him for some reason. Bill came in and signed up Behagen right away. Behagen went on to have a long career in the NBA, but he was the central figure in the brawl on the evening of January 25, 1972.

Ohio State came to Williams Arena for an important game between the top two teams in the Big Ten. In the waning moments of the game (which Ohio State won, 50–44), Ohio State's Luke Witte was fouled hard by Clyde Turner going to the basket. Gophers center Corky Taylor offered his hand to help Witte to his feet and then promptly kneed him in the groin. An all-out melee ensued, and Behagen came off the bench and stomped on Witte's face. Although Taylor and Behagen would be suspended for the rest of the season, Minnesota ended up winning the conference and earning a trip to the NCAA tournament.

Here's how big Gophers basketball was on that January night in 1972: the NHL all-star game was being played at Met Center that same evening, and every sports media person in town, except for the three guys who covered hockey, was at Williams Arena for the Gophers–Buckeyes game.

Saturday afternoons in "the Barn" were fantastic. Gophers basketball became a phenomenon. There were down periods, to be sure, but it was a big attraction from '71 until Clem Haskins left town in 1999.

The season tickets didn't turn over much during those three decades, and the crowd got old. It's amazing how many people started buying season tickets when Musselman came in and still had them until Clem left. Then the school started trying to gouge the season ticket holders for more money, and they lost the loyal audience.

I don't have the fondness for the Barn that I used to. But I do love the elevated floor. Jud Heathcote, the longtime Michigan State coach and one of my all-time favorite guys, wasn't a fan. In fact, in his 1995 autobiography he wrote that he hated Williams Arena "with a passion." When they redesigned the Barn in the early '90s, Jud said, "What idiot decided to keep the raised floor?"

Charley Hallman, the beat writer for the St. Paul paper, asked him, "Why don't you like the elevated floor?"

Jud replied, "If you were an ugly SOB like me—and you are, sir—would you like to be standing up there all by yourself for a whole game with 15,000 people looking at you?"

After Musselman's departure in '75, Jim Dutcher came in and had some great talent to work with. If Mark Olberding and Mark Landsberger had stayed after Musselman left (Olberding left early to play in the American Basketball Association and Landsberger transferred to Arizona State), that 1975–76 Gophers team would have been stacked, with Olberding and Landsberger joining future NBA players Mychal Thompson and Ray Williams, guard Osborne Lockhart, and Flip Saunders as a backup point guard.

Ray Williams was an all-time great—when he was interested in playing. He kicked Indiana's rear a couple of times. He was fantastic. He just didn't get real excited when they were playing a school like Corpus Christi.

Dutcher had a good run as Gophers basketball coach (1975–86), but things blew up for him after rape allegations were made against three of his players following a game in Madison in January '86. All three players were later acquitted, but Dutcher resigned when the administration decided to forfeit the next game at Northwestern.

In the fallout of that mess, very few players had stuck around by the time the university hired Clem Haskins from Western Kentucky to be the new coach before the 1986–87 season. I hardly knew Clem at all when he came to Minnesota, just that he had been a great player back in the mid-'60s.

The Gophers were terrible that first year under Clem. After starting the year 7–3, they lost their last 16 games. I remember him getting misty, almost crying after they beat some nondescript team from a small conference.

My relationship with Clem was a little rough at first. A writer who did investigative pieces for *New York Newsday* was writing an article on college basketball recruiting and cheating. Gophers assistant coach Silas McKinnie had been down in Alabama on a recruiting trip, and he was a character in this investigative piece.

Somebody sent me a copy of this story. I called up Clem to tell him about it. I was going to write something about the story, and I wanted a comment from him.

Clem asked, "Where are you?"

I said, "I'm in the office."

He said, "Stay right there. I'll be there in eight minutes."

Clem drove over, and he brought a couple of columns I had written. He had highlighted in yellow some remarks that he didn't approve of. He showed them to me and said, "I'm not talking about Silas. I'm talking about *this*."

By Clem's third season, the Gophers slipped into the NCAA basketball tournament as an 11 seed and made it to the Sweet 16. I was with the team in Greensboro, North Carolina, for the opening rounds. They upset sixth-seeded Kansas State in the first round, and then they beat 14 seed Sienna in the second round. They lost to Duke in the Sweet 16.

Clem showed that he could coach because he made his players rebound and he made them play defense. The next year they got in the tournament as a six seed and made it to the Elite Eight after beating second-seeded Syracuse. Kevin Lynch missed a three-pointer at the buzzer against Georgia Tech that would have taken them to the Final Four.

I had gotten back on Clem's good side by then. We had total access to this team, Clem and his players, and we got to know them all.

Clem and the Gophers made it to the Final Four in '97, and *Star Tribune* photographer Jerry Holt and I went down to

Campbellsville, Kentucky, to visit Clem's hometown. We went to see his mom, Lucy, and learned about where Clem grew up. Clem had built his own place up the hill from the old family farm. His childhood home now had indoor plumbing, but it didn't when he was a kid.

Lucy was the nicest woman ever, and she was true old south, man. She cooked on a wood-burning stove. As we were getting ready to leave, Lucy said, "Would you boys like some fried apple pie?"

I said, "That's OK. We need to be going."

Jerry, who is from the South, said, "Oh, no. We're staying."

And Jerry made the right call.

I had gotten close to Clem during that time, and the fact that his tenure ended in an academic fraud scandal did not change my opinion of him. When you look back at that situation—a university employee writing papers for some of Clem's players—it doesn't seem like much by today's standards of wrongdoing in college sports. He had his athletes' best interests at heart. A lot of people don't agree with that.

Still, when the Gophers were good, Minnesota loved him. He'd throw off his sport coat when he got mad on the sideline, and the Williams Arena crowd would go crazy. His teams were tough competitors.

But if you were in Clem's doghouse, it was an uncomfortable place to be. And Willie Burton was there often—even though he was by far Clem's most gifted player. Willie is one of my favorite all-time characters, one reason being that Willie loved himself some Willie. He loved to shoot. He didn't love to rebound or play defense. Clem basically turned him into a rebounder.

After freshman year, I think it was, Willie wasn't exactly pounding the books, and he wasn't doing what Clem wanted him to do off the court. Clem was pissed.

According to Willie, Clem brought him down to the Haskins farm in Kentucky when the first crop of hay was coming in. Imagine Kentucky in late June, hotter than Hades. Willie was throwing hay down there for a week, with Clem saying, "Unless you start doing what I tell you, you are going to be back here again next year."

Willie loves Clem. Just loves him. All his players do because he was on their side. The '97 team that made it to the Final Four was a great team, but that first group that reached the Elite Eight in '90 is special. You know what they are? They're the '87 Twins compared to the '91 Twins. The 1996–97 team didn't shock us when they went to the Final Four. The '89 squad shocked us by going to the Sweet 16 and shocked us even more by going to the regional final the next year.

I had some great moments as a reporter going on road trips with the Gophers. On one particular trip, they were traveling to Indiana and then Ohio State. The Gophers let me ride the team bus from Bloomington, Indiana, to Columbus, Ohio.

I sat in the front and Clem was across the aisle. It was late at night, and the bus was quiet and dark. Clem started telling stories about growing up in the South. He was going to be one of the first players to integrate Louisville's basketball program, but then he got homesick and called his mom and said he was coming home. He went home for two weeks and then enrolled at Western Kentucky, which had already been integrated.

He told me another story that brought tears to his eyes. His best buddy at Western Kentucky was Dwight Smith, who was a great player and better than his brother Greg Smith, who ended up having a long NBA career. They also had a sister who Clem said was just the sweetest gal.

The three Smith siblings were driving home late at night from Western Kentucky to see their mom on Mother's Day. It was rainy and icy, and they were on a back road when their car hydroplaned and flipped into a water-filled ditch. Dwight and his sister both drowned in the car. Greg was the lone survivor.

Clem was telling me this story two decades later, and it still devastated him. He was such a good guy. I still love him.

Since Clem's been gone, when have we been excited about Gophers basketball? Things got interesting for a little bit when

Tubby Smith was here (2007–13). But the Gophers have won just two NCAA tournament games since Clem was run off.

Here's something else: We knew all those players under Dutch and Clem because the media was allowed to make them into personalities. Willie Burton, Richard Coffey—go down the roster—we wrote about those guys from a familiar standpoint. We had access to them, and we wrote about the game in a deep way because we could go talk to the players in detail about what happened. You could write something that had meat on it, instead of how it is now: three guys sitting at an interview table in a big room, not wanting to say anything because they've got a university employee standing next to them.

Richard Coffey kicked me in the head during the regionals in New Orleans in '90. He was chasing a ball and flipped over the bench and nailed me with both of his large sneakers. It was on the sports blooper reels for 20 years. I went into the locker room after the game and said, "Jesus Christ, Richard."

He said, "Guess what. Athletic Director Rick Bay came in here at halftime and said he would give me fifty dollars if I did it again."

You think anybody nowadays is going to give you that kind of quote?

The greatest basketball game I ever covered was the Clemson–Gophers game in the '97 Sweet 16, played in San Antonio. Junior guard Eric Harris injured his shoulder during the game and took only one shot. Bobby Jackson got four fouls, but he played almost 50 minutes and carried the Gophers to a double-overtime win.

Minnesota took over San Antonio that weekend. There were 15,000 Gophers fans down there. The city's River Walk was maroon and gold.

That Clemson team was good. Years later, I talked to their coach, Rick Barnes, about the game. He said there were very few games better than that one in his long coaching career. His team was hard-nosed, and Clem's team was hard-nosed. It was a fantastic basketball game.

■ ■ ■

The Minnesota basketball scene changed when the Timberwolves arrived in 1989. We were excited to have an NBA team again. The organization got Mussy to coach those first two seasons. That was fun. The team set an NBA attendance record playing at the Metrodome. It was a big mistake not staying in the Dome a second year. They rushed into building Target Center. But I just don't think the Twin Cities, at its core, is an NBA market.

If you go back to the Minneapolis Lakers, their last title was in '54. That was when it was a nine-team league. We didn't live and die with the Lakers. We didn't live and die with the NBA. The biggest games the Lakers played were exhibitions against the Harlem Globetrotters, when the Globetrotters played serious basketball.

Yeah, it was fun in 2003 and '04 when the Wolves made a run. But even when they were making the playoffs—except that one year when they had Sam Cassell and Latrell Sprewell—you never felt like they had a chance to get to the finals. Balance has always been the league's problem. What made the COVID-rattled 2020–21 season great was that it was one of the few times in my lifetime when the NBA was unpredictable.

Kevin Garnett was an interesting case. He was a great player and a good guy when he was younger, but man, he got bitter. Glen Taylor, owner of the Timberwolves at that time, owns the *Star Tribune*, and everybody thinks we're protecting him. He's a great newspaper owner, by the way. But Garnett's verbal shots at Taylor after he was traded to Boston were ridiculous. KG made the third- or fourth-most money in the history of the NBA, and most of it came from Glen Taylor, and KG's mad at him.

The Timberwolves have been the No. 1 story in town for about three weeks in their 32-year history. But to me, the NBA today is much better than college basketball. The college game has too many teams, and it's too transient, with transfers and one-and-done players leaving for the NBA. And don't get me started on the three-point shot.

Musselman made college basketball big here by winning games 52–50 when every basket was precious. He would face Bobby

Knight's Hoosiers, and it was like watching a freaking hockey game. They had to work hard for every basket.

When the three-point line came in, we had no idea what it would lead to. One of my favorite Gophers ever was Mark Hall, who played here in the late '70s and early '80s—before the three-point shot was in the college game. He would shoot a pull-up 17-footer off the break. Now if he did that, fans would be saying, "Why is he doing that? What's wrong with him? Why not step back and shoot a three?" That style would not fit with today's basketball.

The game of just throwing up three-pointers—I don't like it at all. I really did love basketball as a kid and through most of my adult life. There's no place I'd rather be than Williams Arena from the early '70s to the late '90s. But now I don't care if I go to games or not. I just don't like the modern game.

Harrumph! Harrumph!

9

A CHAMPION FOR WOMEN'S SPORTS

The Title IX federal law that prohibits sex discrimination in education stands as one of the most important developments in modern sports history. That law gave women athletics the necessary support in seeking treatment equal to their male counterparts.

Reusse tiptoed into this new world of sports coverage at first, but in time he became a staunch supporter of women's sports, particularly at the college level, where he discovered some of his favorite athletes ever.

■ ■ ■

At the 1956 Summer Olympics in Melbourne, the men had 24 events in track and field. The women had nine, including four foot races—the 100- and 200-meter dashes, the 80-meter hurdles, and the 4x100-meter relay. The 800-meter distance was added in 1960 and the 400 in 1964. The women's marathon didn't become an Olympic event until 1984. Apparently, the Olympic committee didn't want women running long distances because they thought the women might run too hard and not be able to bear children or some nonsense. It's unbelievable what we got away with in how we treated women athletes.

The fact that women's sports were being dismissed really didn't occur to us men. When I first got into newspapering as a

< 109 >

copy boy in '63, it was just three years after Wilma Rudolph and the Tigerbelles had been the stars in the Rome Olympics, winning three gold medals. But we didn't sit around the office waiting for the women's sports scores to be called in.

Title IX came along in 1972. I was the morning sports editor at the St. Paul paper at the time, and I was totally unqualified for the job. We didn't know what the hell we were going to do with Title IX. *What does this mean? They're going to have college and high school sports with women? They're going to be more than cheerleaders?*

Listen, I'm just telling the truth. I'm not saying it was right. We had a total lack of consciousness about women's sports. The idea that there was such abject discrimination in college and high school athletics wasn't a daily talking point in the American sports media. Of course, many women realized how discriminatory it was.

With Title IX, suddenly we had women's team sports events. And a few years later, the girls high school tournaments started. The newspaper gave big coverage to the girls state basketball tournament. But we still didn't really know what we were dealing with.

Every time I look back at those days, I ask myself: *How did we get away with it? How did the male gender get away with this?*

This revelation has led me to reexamine my early years of covering women's sports, including my battles with Chris Voelz, the women's athletic director at the U from 1988 to 2002. My belief back then was, *Why do we need a women's athletic director? Why can't the school have just one AD like normal?*

Voelz fought for every inch women athletes gained at the university. You look at what the university has today, and you have to realize that she worked really hard to make that happen. She is the one who went out and got a hotshot volleyball coach. She's the one who got Ridder Arena built as the home for the women's hockey team. She's the one who made sure that staffing for women's athletics was equal to what it was for men's athletics.

Damn, she was obnoxious, though. She would fight battles that didn't have to be fought. But looking back, I realize it was the only way forward. She and her staff and the women athletes had to shake us up. They had to shake up the male power structure to say, *Hey, you're not going to get away with it anymore!*

I started feeling this sentiment in the mid-'90s as I got to know and cover more and more women's athletics. The shift in the way we provide opportunity to women in sports is probably the most impactful happening during my sports lifetime.

I visited the University of Connecticut the year we had the Women's Final Four here at Target Center in 1995. Kara Wolters was one of the star players for a dominant UConn team. She was six-foot-seven, six-foot-eight. A big woman.

In previous eras, she would have been the kid who walked the hallways at school stooped over in self-consciousness. Now she was a star on campus. I brought this up with her, and she started crying because her mother never had a similar opportunity.

But I will admit I still wasn't fully on board as attitudes began to change in the '90s. My stance became particularly evident on March 2, 1991, a day that shall live in my personal infamy.

Back then, I would often drive up to the Iron Range in the winter, usually in February or March, to find stories. This time in '91, I was going to go to Duluth to cover a boxing match at the DECC Arena. Michael Moorer was scheduled to fight, but the event was canceled for some reason, so I didn't have a column.

I decided I would just write some cute little observations. My first item was giving Clem Haskins grief about road games. One year in the early '90s when the Gophers went to the National Invitation Tournament, they played two games at Met Center and one at Target Center, and he claimed them as road games, since it wasn't their usual home court at Williams. I compared Clem to Saddam Hussein's PR guy Tariq Aziz, who was always on TV spinning yarns. That was the spirit of the column.

Around that time I had seen a junior college women's basketball game. I can't remember why I was there. And then I watched a high school girls game. A really terrible game.

I had this thought: *Boy, I expected women's basketball would have progressed more than it has. It should be better than this.*

So in my column I referred to women's basketball as "tip-toed ball throwing."

The next day I flew to Florida for the start of Twins spring training. Obviously there was no internet then, so I had no idea what was going on back home, as far as the reaction to my piece.

Meanwhile, my stepson Ryan was a student at Benilde–St. Margaret's. His best friend's sister was a basketball player there. They put my column up in the school hallway and had a target on it. That was happening all over. I was oblivious to it all because I was at spring training.

Finally, I got a call from Joel Kramer—not from Tim McGuire, the editor, but Joel Kramer, who was the boss-boss and soon became the publisher of the paper. I never got calls from Joel Kramer. He told me about the backlash and said I needed to apologize for what I'd written.

I told him I'd be home in a week, and we could figure out something then. I didn't realize the letters were pouring in at the newspaper.

Then Don Shelby, the longtime anchor at WCCO-TV, wrote a piece for the *Star Tribune* editorial page. Don had a daughter or two playing basketball, and he was a big proponent of women's basketball. He wrote a 30-inch column saying, basically, that I should be fired.

I got back to town, and the letters at the office were stacked up to my head. I wrote what I thought was a clever apology column. I offered a response to certain letters, starting with ones that had mild reactions and moving on to those that had more vitriol. By the end of the column, the harshest letters were telling me what a creep I was, and I was begging for mercy. We boldfaced the first letter in each correspondent's note so that if you read down the left side of the column it spelled out, "OK you win."

I submitted the column, and a couple hours later the editors said, "No, that's too flippant." A couple of weeks later I wrote another apology.

I will say, that episode changed me. The late, great Bud Armstrong, a longtime copy desk guy, told me later, "I wish I'd been working the desk that night. I would have saved you a lot of headaches because I would have told you 'No.'"

I did get in trouble again when the women's Final Four was here in '95. Stanford was supposed to win, and UConn drilled them in the semifinals. Stanford played terribly. I wrote, "Now we know why Stanford's mascot is a tree because that's the way they moved on the court."

A couple of women who were working the tournament as volunteers confronted me in the hallway at the arena the next day. My only defense was that if it had been the Stanford men, I would have written the same thing.

Despite these missteps, I've had some great moments covering women's sports. Nothing compares to the 2004 Gophers team that made it to the Final Four. That was great. God, they were good kids. That team had talent and plenty of personality. Lindsay Whalen had a big presence. Janel McCarville might be an all-time, top-five character.

The team had been beyond awful when Whalen came to the U in 2000. Cheryl Littlejohn was the coach. They finished last or tied for last every year that she was there. They were drawing about 200 people a game at the Sports (now Maturi) Pavilion. To see the transformation they made over the next three years, first under coach Brenda Oldfield for one season and then under Pam Borton, was astounding.

I was with the team the whole time during the 2004 tournament. They beat UCLA in front of 14,000 fans in Williams Arena, and those kids were having the time of their lives.

What was great about these players was you'd talk to them and they'd give you good answers. They were funny. I'll never forget McCarville going up against poor Nicole Ohlde from Kansas

State, who was an All-American. K-State was the No. 2 seed in the bracket, but they had to come to Minnesota for the opening weekend of the tournament. The Gophers were the seventh seed because they lost some regular season games after Whalen got hurt.

The refs let them play physical, and McCarville dang near threw Ohlde off the court about three times. The Gophers beat 'em bad, 80–61. The Gophers went to Virginia for the regionals and beat third-seeded Boston College and then beat No. 1 Duke to get to the Final Four in New Orleans.

They became a huge story in town. For all that Lindsay accomplished later with the Minnesota Lynx in the WNBA, this was the moment that lives with her. What a competitor, and what a person. She used to go out to her hometown of Hutchinson, Minnesota, on the weekends and have a couple of beers with her old high school pals.

McCarville comes from the most blue-collar area in Wisconsin, Stevens Point. In 2004 her mother had terminal cancer, and I remember talking to her mom at the regional. Man, what an emotional moment to have that NCAA run with her daughter. It was a great story.

■ ■ ■

The other women's sport I have really gotten into is volleyball. I think volleyball is the best women's sport as far as the athletes you see. A volleyball match has the equivalent of like 30 goal-line stands in football. That's what it feels like. And there are some great people in that sport.

The first volleyball piece I truly loved writing was about Katie Callahan and Heidi Olhausen, in the early '90s. They were two terrific players for the Gophers, and they were both hilarious.

The coach of women's volleyball now, Hugh McCutcheon, has a towering, confident presence, and he's the perfect college coach because all he has to do to get everyone's attention is simply stand up. When he's sitting over by the bench watching the action and then he stands, the players think, *OK, he's going to tell me to do something here, and I better listen because it's going to help us.*

The U's women's programs are their most successful right now. The volleyball team is a top 10 program. The softball team made it to the College World Series in 2019. Their other Olympic sports are successful.

Nationally, Americans still haven't come around completely to women's sports. The 2021 Olympics in Tokyo should help more people recognize the abilities of our women athletes, considering the US women brought home 66 medals while the men won 41.

Back in 2006, I had a fantastic time covering Natalie Darwitz and Krissy Wendell of the US women's hockey team at the Turin Olympics. After one of their wins, I called Natalie on her cell phone as they were riding back to the athletes village. She told me, "I just got a call from Uncle Steve, and he's happy."

Her uncle had been watching the game in a bar on West Seventh in St. Paul. He bet some guys in the bar that he could get an Olympian on the phone. They took him up on it, and he called his niece after the game. He won $50.

The first Winter Olympics I covered were in Calgary in '88. The Olympics had gotten a new TV contract, and they made the events extend over 16 days and three weekends. But the problem was, the events were still scheduled on the old 10-day schedule from previous Olympics. There were many days when nothing was going on.

The big story that year was figure skating, especially Brian Boitano from the United States and Brian Orser from Canada. In the women's field, Debi Thomas was the first prominent African American skater to compete for the United States. She was the US darling. And Katarina Witt was the great German and defending Olympic gold medalist. Elizabeth Manley was a big star from the host country of Canada.

I covered a lot of figure skating that year. I knew nothing about the sport, but I saw more figure skating than I had seen in my life that week. I went to all the preliminaries. There were some great characters. There was a competitor from England named Joanne

Conway, who seemed to be a nice person, but I started calling her "Crash Conway" because she would get out there and start banging into the boards. I kind of had fun with it.

Figure skating had a scoring system that went up to six—6.0 being perfect. It was scored by tenths, but the judges could put only one competitor at each score. So there could be only one 5.8, one 5.6, and so on. It was really weird for a guy who was raised on touchdowns and extra points.

Katarina got, I believe, a 5.8, so it appeared the judges were saving the 5.9 and, potentially, the gold medal for Debi Thomas.

But poor Debi got out there and fell down a couple of times. She skated terribly and took the bronze medal. I wrote in my column that "Debi choked." Several dozen letters of complaint were sent to the St. Paul paper. You were not supposed to demean the competitors, especially in figure skating, and certainly not Debi.

There were several columnists like me who knew nothing about figure skating but had to write about it. They were all stealing their insights from Dick Button, the US television analyst. I knew what everybody was up to, so I'd listen to the Canadian broadcast and steal from them.

It was fun. I liked it. Plus, I had a lot of fun with Katarina's beauty. It became a radio bit, how jealous I was that she was running around with Alberto Tomba, the studly, gorgeous skier from Italy. They were the couple in Calgary.

Not long after those Olympics, I switched newspapers and was out of action for two weeks between jobs. The bit on the radio became that I was off running away with Katarina. Later on, she was in town for an event or something. I wasn't around, but she came to the Hubbard Broadcasting building for a TV interview with KSTP, and they got her to do a greeting on the radio: "Hey, Patrick, I've missed you."

Three years after Calgary, the US Figure Skating Championships were held at Target Center. It was an impressive field of competitors. Kristi Yamaguchi was already a big star, and Nancy Kerrigan was on the rise.

And, of course, there was Tonya Harding, who was known as an athletic skater but was certainly not considered the favorite to win. But she became the first American woman to land a triple axel in competition and won first place. That put her on the map, and then she finished fourth at the '92 Olympics.

The trials for figure skating to determine the 1994 Olympic team were held in Detroit in January of that year. Jay Weiner was covering the event for the *Star Tribune*. Jay always told the story about the day that somebody frantically ran into the pressroom during practice and said, "Nancy Kerrigan just got hit in the ankle with a blunt object."

Jay said everybody in the room turned around and said, "Tonya."

Harding did not have the typical figure skating upbringing. If Allison Janney's portrayal of Harding's mom in the movie *I, Tonya* was true to life, I wouldn't be surprised. Harding's story is an amazing one that would be a great American tale—if not for the fact that her buddies hit Nancy Kerrigan with a pipe.

Harding had to sue to get on the '94 Olympic team. The US Olympic Committee was not going to send her to Lillehammer for the Winter Olympics. She was still under criminal investigation, but nothing had been proven yet, so they let her go.

The skating arena in Lillehammer had a practice rink next to it. It was a small hockey rink, smaller than St. Paul's Aldrich Arena. On the first day of the US team's practice, there had to have been 500 of us reporters standing there waiting to see what would happen when Tonya and Nancy crossed paths. You never saw two people work as hard to stay away from each other as they did on the ice that day.

Tonya had a bad ankle, and she would cry after a jump because her ankle hurt. The Olympics turned into a disaster for her, and her life pretty much did too.

The pre-competition press conference with the entire US team was absolutely jam-packed with media. A clip of me in the crowd holding my fat chin somehow made the highlights and still gets shown a lot. It was the weirdest press conference imaginable.

Tonya certainly made figure skating more interesting. It was one of those 10 stories that you run into in a lifetime of journalism that you just can't believe. You're like, *What?! She got hit with a metal pipe walking down to practice?* Just unbelievable.

■ ■ ■

Of course, we can't mention women's sports without talking about our Lynx. They've won four WNBA championships and had some of the all-time great players in that sport's history.

What Maya Moore did for that organization was unbelievable. The UConn star was drafted by the Lynx in 2011, and they won four titles in seven years, beginning with her rookie season. She's the figure who made the franchise.

One thing I would like to see in women's basketball is for not all the best players to go to UConn. UConn has the first- and second-best teams in the country, and that's not right. You could have a WNBA All-Star Game of just former UConn players.

I do have a good story relating to UConn's Rebecca Lobo, their big star from the early '90s. She married my pal Steve Rushin, a Bloomington, Minnesota, guy who is one of the greatest in the history of American sportswriting, and a fine fellow. He told me that he used to ride his bike to the corner store to get the *St. Paul Dispatch* when I was writing columns for that paper. I'd now ride my bike to the corner store to read Rushin.

I saw Rebecca at Williams Arena one night when she was in town as a broadcaster covering women's basketball for ESPN. I went over and introduced myself and told her that I was her husband's idol. She looked at me like I was nuts.

Then, in April 2005, I was in Columbus, Ohio, covering the Gophers at the NCAA hockey Frozen Four. Rushin was there too. I went over to him and said, "You know, I told your wife that I was your idol, and she dismissed it out of hand." He said, "Well, we'll take care of that."

He called her on his cell phone and said, "You should apologize to my friend Pat Reusse for doubting that he is my idol." She got on the phone, and we talked for a few minutes. She's a great person as well as a Hall of Fame basketball player.

Anyway, it is a phenomenon of my lifetime that we treated women's sports the way we did. It is never too late to apologize again for my "tip-toed ball throwing" comment.

10

"WE TOOK IT VERY IRREVERENTLY"

Reusse found success and longevity as a multimedia personality long before that became a popular career path for modern sports journalists. Minnesotans know Reusse as much for his deep, gravelly voice that occasionally pitches up several octaves when he is in the middle of telling a story on the radio as they do his work in print as a newspaper columnist.

A sports talk radio pioneer in Minnesota, Reusse established a cult following as part of his radio show with Joe "Sooch" Soucheray and a roundtable sports television show featuring a cast of characters. His work in those media earned Reusse a spot in the Minnesota Broadcasting Hall of Fame in 2019.

■ ■ ■

In 1980, KSTP-1500 transformed itself from a general news station to a news-talk station with call-in shows. A guy named Art Schreiber was in charge of that transformation as the station manager. Artie decided the station should have a sports talk show every night. At first they had sportswriters do it. Dan Stoneking had two nights, Joe Soucheray had one, Doug Grow had one, and Bruce Brothers had one. Then, the capable Gene Harrington did the show on Saturday nights. I was invited to be a part, but the

< 121 >

St. Paul paper wouldn't let me do it. From the get-go, it was obvious that Sooch was the best of the radio crew.

Sooch and I were pretty tight by then. When he first came aboard as a sportswriter in the mid-'70s, he was from a different planet than us hard-core sports guys. In 1974 we were in New York together for a Twins–Yankees game. It was the 14th inning, and Joe was screaming that the Twins weren't using Tony Oliva as a pinch hitter. I had to remind Sooch that Tony left the game in the eighth and they couldn't bring him back in.

Sooch actually benefitted from the fact that he wasn't a huge sports guy. Everything that was so routine for those of us who had followed sports our whole lives was different for Joe. He would make interesting observations about things that we just took for granted. And he was a great writer too.

In '81 the St. Paul paper told me I could do the radio show. KSTP put me on Sunday nights. It was for three hours, six to nine. I had zero experience. We begged for phone calls to help fill the time.

Then the station hired Ted Robinson, who became a nationally prominent announcer, to do the sports show Monday through Friday. They kept Harrington for Saturday. And they wanted to keep Sooch, so they put him with me on Sunday.

Right away, we were a wacky team. We took it very irreverently. We made fun of Bud Grant and stuff like that. We were a call-based show and didn't have guests. On one particular summer Sunday, we couldn't get any calls, and we threatened to stand on the table until we got calls. People started calling in.

We lasted about a year. In the spring of 1982 a guy came in as the new station manager and got rid of the two shows that were costing him the most money. That included our show, even though Joe and I were making just $30 an hour. Ninety bucks apiece per week. We were done, and our reaction was, *That was free money for a year.*

Then a guy named Scott Meier came in as the program director, and he told us, "We want you to do a Monday night show called

Monday Night Sports Talk." It was September of '83. He offered us the kingly sum of $50 an hour for two hours, and Sooch and I said, "When do we start?"

We had characters who would call in to the show regularly. Greg Harrington, Gene's kid, was quite the impersonator, and he ignited it all with his whining Neal Broten voice. He also could do a good Lou Nanne lisp. And he did Frank Quilici as the Q Man. Harrington's Q Man praising a player for his machismo was priceless. Then Guy Green became Harrington's foil and cohort with his own world-class impersonations, particularly of Lou Holtz. Guy Green and Harrington had a spin-off show for a while on Tuesday nights.

All these bits kind of took over the show. We had these kids from White Bear Lake who called themselves "Toads"—Terrorists Organized Against Disgusting Sports. They were 16- or 17-year-olds, and they would call up and do these shticks. They didn't like one of the local sportscasters, and one time they had a whole skit about how they kidnapped him, and they had fireworks going off in the background.

We had another caller, the Walker Pilot Independent guy. He had this gentle voice, and he'd call up and read the news out of the Walker *Pilot* paper each week. You know, "Gladys Schwartz had three people over for coffee" and stuff like that.

It got completely out of control. It just became this cult thing. I still have people coming up to me and saying, "I go back to Sunday Night."

Elmer and his wife from Elko would call in with some adventure they'd had that week. A guy who called himself Bill Quilici would do whole routines about being Frank's imaginary brother. Another guy would call in and just say, "Orange pop." That's all he'd say. Now he's like 55 years old with kids, but he used to call our show and say, "Orange pop." And we would say, "What was that, sir?" And he'd say, "Orange pop." He never said hello or goodbye.

It would be hard to name all the different characters who called, but they created the show—the callers, not us. It was a crazy, whacked-out show. We were in our 30s at the time. We didn't mind acting like idiots.

The show was really hot for seven, eight years. Then we added another show on Saturday mornings that was more sports-heavy. That really was a good show, *Saturday Morning Sports Talk.*

Joe got his own show in '93, *Garage Logic.* We kept both the Monday and Saturday shows going for a while, then we dropped Monday and kept Saturday.

We were still on Monday nights when Dark Star called in. I didn't know him then. Never heard of him.

For some background, when Bud Grant quit the Vikings after the '83 season, he gave the big scoop to Sid. Now it's early December 1985, and Bud is finishing up another season back as coach after a year away. A guy called our show and said, "This is Dark Star." He said, "Bud Grant is going to quit again." We started going, "We got it! We got the scoop! Bud's quitting! We got it from Dark Star. What other source do you need?"

We had no idea who this guy was. As it turned out, Dark got the scoop from Mike Lynn's brother Robert while drinking with him at the Lafayette Club on Lake Minnetonka. He called us immediately.

The Vikings denied it. Sid robustly denied it. Then, a few days after the season, Bud announced he was quitting again. Sooch and I said: "Sid's days are over. We now have a new scoop monster in town: Dark Star." Sooch wrote a column about Dark Star in the St. Paul paper.

Soon I had the privilege of meeting Dark Star. His whole thing in life was to become somebody, to become known.

His dad was one of the founders of Gelco Leasing, and Dark was working leasing cars. Next to radio, nothing fit Dark better than the car business. He was made for it.

Allegedly, Dark Star's nickname comes from the horse that was the upset winner of the Kentucky Derby in 1953. (His real name was George Chapple.) According to him, he was living in California before relocating to the Twins Cities and claimed to have been one of the horse handicappers at the LA *Herald Examiner.*

By '86 and '87 Canterbury racetrack in Shakopee was cranking it up, really packing people in. Each newspaper had a lead handicapper and a handicap box with three other handicappers in there. When the lead handicapper for the *Pioneer Press* got taken off the beat and one of the three in the box moved to lead handicapper, we needed another guy in the box.

The sports editor was in a panic. I told him I might know someone. I called Dark and said, "Have you ever been to a horse race in your life, or is it all b.s.?" He said, "Nah, I'm great."

I said, "Do you want to be in the *Pioneer Press* selection box?" He said, "Hell, yes."

Dark called in his picks on Tuesday for Wednesday's card. Then he called back on Tuesday night after he had been at the bar with the trainers and changed about three of his picks. I went to the track on Wednesday to proudly stand with my discovery, and he went 0-for-9 the first day.

Suddenly, two weeks later, he was on Steve Cannon's drive-time show on WCCO giving him the report from Canterbury about what happened that day.

Then Dark got the *Dark Star Show* on KANO in Anoka. He would record in the middle of the week at a sports bar. He was working me over to come up to Anoka to be a guest on his show.

I drove there through traffic and arrived just in the nick of time. Turns out, Dark was filling in on 'CCO that night. I was the guest on the *Dark Star Show*, hosted by Bill Ward. Dark had never told me he wasn't going to be there. What a beauty he was.

Dark Star became somebody in this town by calling our show and correctly saying Bud Grant was going to quit again. I don't think Sid ever forgave him for that; those two guys never got along.

When Dark died in 2012, a guy came up to me—I think it was his accountant—and said, "Dark said you and he were like brothers. You were the brother he never had." I was proud of that, even though I know Dark probably said that same thing about 30, 40 other guys.

No, we were really close. I just loved him. His attitude was, *What can I get away with today?*

In 1991 somehow the North Stars made it into the Stanley Cup Finals, despite having a losing record that season. It was a terrible team. At Met Center, their home arena, owner Norm Green built a booth in one corner where he could stand like Nero, waving to the crowd. As soon as Dark saw that, you knew he wanted to get in that booth.

I got along great with Norm. He'd call me when they were drawing 4,000 fans and ask, "What am I going to do?" I'd tell him, "Norm, you're talking to the wrong guy. I don't know anything about hockey."

But the North Stars made it to the Stanley Cup Finals in '91, and then Norm put the home games on pay-per-view, and only 35 percent of the Twin Cities could even buy the telecast. I wrote a column calling him "Norm Greed" and ripping the hell out of him.

They won Game 3 at home, and they were leading the Stanley Cup finals 2–1. The crowd was chanting, "Norm, Norm," and he was waving to them.

After finishing my piece on the game, I tuned in to Dark's show on my drive home, like usual, to hear what he was talking about. The topic for the day was, "Does the Twin Cities really need a negative sports columnist like Patrick Reusse?"

Everybody calling in was saying, "Get rid of that fat SOB. I never liked him. He's terrible."

I had Dark's direct number at the station, and I called him during a commercial break. I said, "Hey, that's quite a show you got going there tonight, Dark."

He replied, "Ain't it great? They fucking hate you! I might do this again tomorrow night, it's so good."

I think the greatest moment of Dark Star's life was when he sat at the table with Chuck Knoblauch when Knobby signed with the Twins in 1996. Dark had befriended Knobby and became the middleman, in his view, in getting him signed.

Knobby gave him credit for helping make it possible. The press conference was at the Metrodome. Knobby's agent, Twins general manager Terry Ryan, and Dark were sitting up at the front table. Dark was so damn happy, not only because of the attention it brought him but because he knew it drove Sid crazy. Sid was so competitive that he wanted every scoop and hated it when somebody else got news before him. That was the end for Dark and Sid.

Anyway, the radio show matured, but we still had fun. One bit Joe and I did was to go off about the exotic spellings of baby names. You know, parents would give their kid a different spelling of the name Christina, for example. Then parents started naming kids after weather conditions and stuff like that. We called it doodling. Joe would get very upset about doodled first names. On the show, we'd read off these names and say whether or not we approved.

People started calling in to the show to say, "Hey, we just had a baby and we named it 'such and such,'" and they'd ask for our approval. Then, when we did our radio show live at the state fair, we started the "Baby Walk": during the second hour of the show people would bring up their babies to see if we approved of their names.

One year we had 140 babies—so many that we had to keep going after the show ended. If it was a marginal name and we gave it approval, the crowd would boo and heckle the parents. We had mothers give us the middle finger if we didn't sign off on their baby's name. The whole thing was hysterical and became incredibly popular with listeners.

When we started doing our Saturday radio show, everybody said that nobody listens to the radio on Saturday morning. But we found out a lot of guys were going to Menards or taking their wife someplace and they stayed out in the car.

Our preparation for each morning's show was consistent—none. Sometimes Joe wasn't there when the opening music started.

I would usually get there two minutes before 10. Our show started at 10:05 because the news ran before we got on. Then they would play the song "I Heard It Through the Grapevine" as a lead-in to our show. Sometimes we were on the second go-round of the song before Joe walked in.

I would say 80 percent of the time we never said who we were or the name of the show, simply because it never occurred to us. Nobody knew what the topic was going to be. We just started, "You know what irritated me this week . . . " I think the spontaneity was the secret of our success.

Joe finally wore out doing five shows a week of *Garage Logic* and then doing our show. So Judd Zulgad started doing Saturdays with me in 2010.

In 2009 I took a weekday morning show. I loved it, but it damn near killed me. That show lasted 13 months. Then KSTP-1500 became an all-sports station, and I had a daily show that lasted through 2018.

Once you get to be 60 years old, laughing like an idiot all day long is not quite as good as it was when you first started. I still say the first five or six years of *Monday Night Sports Talk* were my favorite, hard to beat. And we had very little to do with it. We just encouraged it.

The Hubbard family—of Hubbard Broadcasting, which owned the station—were great people. Even when our show ended in 2018, they were really generous. The Hubbards are also well-known for being on the right side of the political spectrum. I was an outspoken lefty but never heard a word about it.

Joe and I had Rush Limbaugh on the show twice. I said, "Rush, that's a good bit you got going." He got very upset at me. After Joe started doing *Garage Logic*, we had Rush on again, and later we had Sean Hannity. I didn't talk politics that much on the show, but if I did, I poked people.

Once Joe had me fill in for him on *Garage Logic*. During the broadcast, I said, "I'll never forget the time Rush and I were eating together in Kansas City in the lunchroom"—he used to work for the Royals—"Two fat guys. We eat a little longer than everybody else. We start b.s.-ing, and Rush says, 'I've got to figure out a way to make more money. You know I'm a pretty liberal guy, but the people that can really be duped are the conservatives.'"

Well, scores of Rush fans ended up contacting his office to report me. A day later, his representatives were threatening to leave the station if I didn't go on and say it was a joke. Of course it was a joke.

Back to my work with Sooch, I don't know how our personalities fit so well. Joe's a very private guy, and I tell stories about flaws. We're very different. He's much better on radio. I'm strictly off-the-cuff. The show never would have made it without him.

■ ■ ■

The Sports Show TV program happened because Dark Star was a big admirer of the *Sports Writers on TV* show out of Chicago. It was a bunch of guys sitting around smoking cigars and talking about sports. Dark thought it could be done here. And it was a chance to make a little money.

Dark had become buddies with WCCO's Mike Max. They went and pitched the show idea to what was then Midwest Sports Channel. The way Dark told the story, Maxie said, "I'll get Sid," and Dark said, "I'll get Reusse," which was him calling me up and saying, "Do you want to do a TV show?"

Dark and Maxie were responsible for hustling up the sponsors. Heck, I made $300 a week for a half-hour's work for 20 years doing that show. It was the deal of a lifetime. And talk about lack of show prep—that show was the champion. God, we had fun though.

For about two years I would bring my yellow Lab, Stout, into the studio for tapings. People loved that dog. One Sunday afternoon I was in the office writing something, and my phone rang. A man said, "Reusse, is the dog going to be on tonight?"

I said, "I don't think so."

He said, "I'm not watching then," and he hung up the phone.

The animosity between Dark and Sid on the show was not an act. There were about three days a year where those two would be nice to each other. Sid couldn't stand Dark because Dark didn't kiss the ring. Maxie would agitate Sid too, but he'd kiss the ring when push came to shove.

A couple times a month Maxie would come up with some fable about a party he had been at with prominent people in town. He would direct the story to Dark and me knowing that it would get a reaction out of Sid. And Sid could think of nothing else during the next segment because he was worried about why he didn't get invited to the party. Maxie was great at agitating him.

The best ever was after the 1998 Winter Olympics, when Maxie asked, "What did you think about Tara Lipinski?" She had just won the gold medal in figure skating at age 15. Youngest ever. Just an amazing thing.

Maxie asked about Lipinski, and Sid said, "I don't know anything about Clinton and that woman."

The next day I went to the Strib offices and got a picture of Tara Lipinski skating and put Monica Lewinski's head on her. We showed that photo on the next Sunday's show.

Another time, Sid started screaming at me about how I didn't really know George Steinbrenner. Apparently, something had reminded him of how I used to rip Steinbrenner, the controversial Yankees owner.

I said, "Sid, you took me to breakfast with him last year when we were in Tampa for a Vikings game. In fact, George and I became buddies. I watched the Olympic swimming with him at the outdoor pool in Barcelona"—which actually had happened.

Sid said, "You went swimming with Steinbrenner?"

That's when I got a picture of two synchronized swimmers, and I put my head on one and George's head on the other. I showed the photo the next Sunday and said, "Sid, here: this is evidence that I went swimming with George."

The Sports Show ran for about 20 years. It was unbelievable. Sunday nights were the perfect time slot. It had a cult following.

One time at spring training in 2018 or '19, I went up to introduce myself to Ryan LaMarre, who was a backup outfielder for the Twins. He said, "I know you."

"How?" I asked him.

He said, "*The Sports Show*. My in-laws in Edina never miss it. When I first started watching it, I thought it was the dumbest ever. Eventually they started taping it for me."

The radio and TV work was a tremendous amount of fun over the years. I know a lot of people do impersonations of me from those shows. There is no doubt that I have a distinctive, growly voice. The secret is the pauses. If you get the pauses down, you're pretty good. Chad Ostlund, once Red McCombs's right-hand man with the Vikings and later Dan Cole's "Our Reusse" on KFAN, is the champion in this regard.

I had a bad throat when I was a kid, to the point that my mother sent me to this woman named Stella in the Twin Cities to take voice lessons. Stella was an opera singer and was supposed to teach me how to speak from my diaphragm. I would stay overnight on a Saturday at this house. I'm not sure if there was a side business there, or something. I was pretty young, so I did not appreciate it fully, but there were a bunch of women running around in lingerie. The lessons didn't really help my voice. Maybe I was too distracted and wasn't paying attention to what Stella was trying to teach me.

11

◆

TEAMMATES WITH SID

Reusse served as Sid Hartman's copy boy as a teenager, then returned to the Minneapolis Star Tribune *two decades later to be Sid's colleague as a general assignment columnist. Their relationship involved ups and downs, many memorable moments in the office and press boxes around the Twin Cities, and more than a few pranks pulled on Sid—which Patrick may or may not have had a hand in.*

■ ■ ■

One of the most common questions I get is about how Sid and I got along. That's a complicated answer.

When I first started at the Minneapolis papers as a copy boy in the mid-'60s, I got a quick introduction to the importance of showing up. Sundays were usually a bit slow at the paper, and one particular Sunday I thought it wouldn't be a big deal if I didn't go in. I learned some valuable lessons that day.

It was a gorgeous fall Sunday in late September, and my buddies were having a beer party out in a guy's pasture in Prior Lake. I called in sick to work: "I can't make it; I'm not feeling well." I wanted to drink beer with the fellas.

At about 4:30 in the afternoon, we saw somebody driving down the path toward the party. We thought it was a cop, so we started

< 133 >

hiding the keg. It was actually the farmer whose land we were on, and he asked, "Is there a Patrick Reusse here?" I said, "Yeah, that's me." He said, "Sid Hartman called and said you're supposed to call him immediately."

How Sid knew I was in that pasture, I'll never know. But the incident taught me two things: 1) Sid Hartman could get anybody on the telephone, anywhere in the world, and 2) Don't call in sick. I never called in sick again. I would have to be near death's door, and I never got that far.

Anyway, that was my first experience with Sid.

Sid was instrumental in helping me develop my philosophy of covering sports. I was still a copy boy in '65 when Norm Van Brocklin suddenly quit one morning as Vikings coach. The team had a disappointing loss in the middle of the season. Presumably, he went home, started drinking, got morbid, and decided, *I've taken this team as far as I can. I quit.*

Sid and Charlie Johnson, who was the executive sports editor and Sid's boss—although Sid didn't really have a boss—happened to be next to my desk that day. They were calling Van Brocklin every derogatory name in the book. They couldn't stand him. Then they both wrote columns pleading for Van Brocklin to return, which he did. I remember thinking to myself, *If I ever get into this business and I think someone is a complete weenie, I'm not going to write that he isn't. I might not write that he is, but I'm not going to write that he isn't.*

That was basically my first dose of Sid. Soucheray also has a great story about getting hired at the *Tribune*. It was 1974 and Larry Batson had become the sports editor. Sid was no longer in charge. He was just writing his five columns a week and trying to run the department even though he wasn't the sports editor. Sooch got hired because Batson had read something of his in an airline magazine. Batson thought it was great, and he wanted to bring in a guy with a different look at sports.

Sooch's first day at the paper was a Sunday. He put on a suit and tie. He went in, and there was nobody there. He was just sitting around, not sure what the hell he was supposed to do. Then Sid came rolling in at about four in the afternoon. He sat down and started pounding away at the typewriter on his cluttered desk. Sooch finally got up the nerve to go and introduce himself. Sid looked up and said, "Hey, horse's ass, how do you spell 'music'?"

I left to go to the Duluth paper at the end of 1965. I came back to the Twin Cities to work for the St. Paul paper in '68, but I didn't have a lot to do with Sid until I started covering baseball in '74.

It's astounding how Sid had this town wired up for so many years. In '73 the story was that general manager Jim Finks was leaving the Vikings because he was in a feud with owner Max Winter. Finks wanted to buy five percent of the team, and Max wouldn't sell it to him.

Sid and Max were joined at the hip. The odds of Max not being in Sid's daily column were slim.

Sid loved Finks too. Finks was a great guy. Very popular. The Vikings were a more professional operation when he became general manager. That Winter–Finks dispute was tough for Sid because Max was his longtime buddy.

Bernie Ridder, the owner and publisher of the St. Paul paper, was one of the partners in the Vikings ownership group. Bernie told Ralphie Reeve, who was our Vikings beat writer in St. Paul, that Finks was leaving. I was running the *Pioneer Press* desk that night. I asked Ralphie if he had the scoop ready, and Ralphie said, "I've got to get a quote from Finks before I run it."

I told him, "Ralphie, don't call Finks. If you call Finks, he'll call Sid." Ralphie had a great relationship with Finks. He insisted on calling him. He said, "He won't call Sid. He won't do that to me." I said, "Yes, he will. He's going to call Sid because he would rather have you angry at him than Sid, who would rag him for the rest of his life."

Ralphie called Finks, and Finks called Sid and told him. Both papers had the story the next morning. That's how powerful Sid was.

Sid also knew everybody in the Big Ten. The way the paper covered the conference back then, Sid was tighter with the Iowa guys than he was with some of the Gophers coaches. He had access to every coach and athletic director in the Big Ten. He was particularly tight with Iowa's longtime coach and athletic director Forest Evashevski.

Jon Roe told stories about going to Michigan with Sid, when they'd just burst into Bo Schembechler's office, and the secretary would yell, "You can't go in." And Sid marched in and Bo would give him a big hug.

The great mystery of Sid is how a man with the social graces of a dictator, who couldn't carry on a conversation about anything beyond money and sports, could have all these close relationships with people throughout the sports world.

People always said that Sid couldn't spell but he could figure out compound interest on the fly. He was a financial genius. He used to include things in his column that were outside the sports beat. It might be a little item from the business world. He was the first reporter to mention that some guys who had worked at UNIVAC and Honeywell were starting a company called Control Data in the Twin Cities.

One day in 2020 spring training, about seven months before Sid died at age 100, I was down in Fort Myers working in the press box. The players hadn't arrived in town yet. I was there early. I walked by the office of the Twins PR boss Dustin Morse, and he was on the phone. I heard him say, "Yes, I will try. I'll give it my best shot." The door was open, and I looked in and said, "Sid?" He shook his head yes. Sid would not take "I'll try my best" for an answer. He wanted "Yes," and he practically wanted it notarized when it came to getting guests for his Sunday radio show on WCCO.

That Sunday show was huge, and all Sid wanted was to have the guests. He prepared no questions to ask. He had no particular alley that he wanted to go down. He just wanted to be able to say that he had them on.

After he broke his hip in late 2016, Sid was up and about just two and a half weeks later to go to the press conference introducing P. J. Fleck as the new coach of Gophers football. He just had to be there and get P. J. to make a commitment to appear week after week on Sid's Sunday morning show.

Sid was the most persistent, insistent, obnoxious guy on the telephone trying to get a news item or a guest lined up for his radio show.

■ ■ ■

I worked in St. Paul from 1968 to 1988 and came to the *Star Tribune* in June 1988. Whether it was two decades in St. Paul or three decades back in Minneapolis, my relationship with Sid never changed. When it came to news or opinion with Sid, you were the enemy. He always wanted to beat his own colleagues in getting news. And if he disagreed with your premise for a column, he would let you know.

We were the feisty underdogs in St. Paul, and I loved to agitate Sid. One example of this was around the time that Hayden Fry became the head coach of Iowa football.

Jerry Burns had been the Iowa coach years earlier. As good a coach as he was, Burnsie started what became a 19-year run of the Hawkeyes being .500 or worse. They were terrible for a long time before Hayden Fry got there in '79.

One day I was in the Memorial Stadium press box working on a sidebar. They announced that Fry's Iowa Hawkeye team was leading some really good non-conference opponent at halftime. Sid was four people down from me. We were packed in there tightly. I turned to the guy next to me and said loud enough for Sid to hear, "Boy, Hayden is really doing a good job turning this Iowa team around since Burnsie screwed up the program."

I didn't know Burnsie then—I love him now—but I knew that Sid loved him. Well, here he came, climbing over chairs and bodies to tell me what a jackass I was.

The St. Paul paper hired Charley Walters when I was there. Loel

Schrader was the sports editor, and he got Charley to start his notes column for one reason: to have somebody to compete with Sid on a daily basis. Charley did a good job with that.

Bob Stein was the Timberwolves president when the franchise started in 1989. Sometime in the early years, Charley had a note from Stein—nothing earth-shattering, but Sid didn't like the fact that Charley had it. One day, an intern said to Sid, "You got a call here from Bob Stein." Sid got on the phone and just started bad-mouthing Stein. He basically threatened to run the Timberwolves out of town.

Sid's son, Chad, knew a lot of professional athletes, especially from traveling with the Timberwolves as their radio guy, and he said that his dad was the most competitive person he ever met in his life. He was right. If we had a beat writer getting too many scoops, Sid would tell the team, "Don't talk to him. Talk to me."

We can't talk about Sid without mentioning the pranks. Dennis Brackin covered the Twins and later became an assistant sports editor for the *Star Tribune*. He spent half his time trying to unearth and cover news, and the other half trying to think up pranks, most of them aimed at Sid.

The greatest ever was a prank he played when we were still in the old building on Portland Avenue in downtown Minneapolis. Late one night, a woman who worked a night shift on the desk was confronted by some guy as she was walking to her parking spot in the back of the lot across the street. After that, the company decided it was going to change all the parking spots. Every employee had to send a message to the company with their shift information. The idea was that people who worked at night, particularly women, would get spots up front near the building.

Sid used to park at an angle in the first spot, right in front. He had a better parking spot than handicapped people. Brackin somehow knew how to duplicate someone else's signature on the bottom of our messaging system, so he and I composed a message to Sid. We wrote, "Mr. Hartman, you failed to file for a new parking spot, and all of the spots at the main building have now been assigned. You no longer have a designated spot there. But fortunately, we have found you a new spot at the Heritage Printing Plant over on Plymouth. It won't be too inconvenient because a shuttle bus runs every half hour."

Brackin signed it from Vic, the parking supervisor. It was one of those days when we were done with our work, but we had to wait around to see Sid's reaction. Sid arrived at the office, and six minutes later he came bursting through his door, headed to the publisher's office. He was halfway down the hall as Brackin chased after him, yelling, "Sid! Sid! Stop!"

Another classic is from the 1988 season, after the Twins won the '87 World Series. Three weeks into the season, the team traded Tom Brunansky to St. Louis for Tommy Herr because manager Tom Kelly wanted a second baseman and a No. 2 hitter. The trade proved to be a disaster.

Herr signed with Philadelphia the next year, and when he was back in St. Louis for a series against the Cardinals, the paper there asked him what had happened in Minneapolis. Herr said, "Well, I got there and the big guy at the newspaper misquoted me about being unhappy about being traded to Minnesota." He never identified "the big guy" by name. Sid responded publicly to Herr, stating, "Well, I have that on tape, Mr. Herr."

I said to Brackin, "Is there some fun we can have with this?" We decided we'd convince Sid that Herr was referring to Charley Walters when he mentioned "the big guy."

Paul Hagen, a Hall of Fame baseball writer from the *Philadelphia Daily News*, was a pal of mine. I called Paulie and asked him to get Phillies letterhead and type a message, allegedly from Herr, that read, "Sorry for the misunderstanding, Sid. I always had respect for you. When I referred to the big guy at the newspaper I was talking about Charley Walters."

Not only did Hagen do that, but he got Herr to sign it. Then he mailed it directly to Sid. The next Sunday, Sid said on the radio that he got a letter of apology from Tommy Herr. But he didn't admit that Herr said it was a misunderstanding and that the big guy was actually Walters.

That was a pretty damn good one.

Another great one was when Sid received the Curt Gowdy Media Award from the Naismith Memorial Basketball Hall of Fame in 2003. He got the award as the writer, and "Hot Rod" Hundley, the longtime radio and TV guy for the Utah Jazz, got it as the broadcaster. The Salt Lake City paper, the *Salt Lake Tribune*, wrote like 80 inches on Rod Hundley getting the award, and we wrote two paragraphs on Sid.

Brackin and I printed out the Salt Lake story and put it on the wall outside Sid's office. It was so long that the story went down one side and back up the other. Then we put up our two paragraphs on Sid.

We made a sign that read: "Local newspapers react to Hall of Fame inductees." We had eight feet of Rod Hundley story. Next to it, we had three inches for Sid's. He arrived at his office, looked at the wall, and headed immediately to sports editor Glen Crevier to complain about our lack of coverage about his big honor.

The Ira Berkow story is one of my favorites too. Ira, a young, brilliant writer, a true wordsmith, came to work for the *Minneapolis Tribune* in 1965. Sid put him on the copy desk, and he was the most ill-fitted copy editor of all time. His immense talent was as a writer. Sid didn't want a wordsmith.

The paper sent Ira to the Kentucky Derby one year. Ira's hero—like everyone else's—was Red Smith. Ira wanted to write something offbeat with descriptive prose, in the spirit of his hero. So he went to a farm in Kentucky and found Citation and "interviewed" him about what it was like to win the derby.

At the time, Sid had no travel budget except for football. He had been complaining bitterly about having to waste some of his department's travel budget to send a writer to the Kentucky Derby. He was pacing in the office. Back then we used a Western Union machine, and the operator would hit a bell when they were sending a story to signal to the newsroom that something was coming in.

Sid heard the *ding, ding, ding,* and he leapt up from his desk and went over to the machine. We could hear him grumbling. We were all watching because everybody was anticipating his reaction to Berkow's story. Finally, he said, "I knew this was a mistake. The son of a bitch interviewed a horse."

Another time Ira was doing a Twins sidebar about a game in which the Twins fell behind and came back, fell behind and came back. Ira's lede to his story was about how it was like Sisyphus pushing the rock up the hill. Sid saw that and said, "Sisyphus, who does he play for?"

■ ■ ■

Tim McGuire was the editor when I came back to the *Star Tribune* as a columnist. McGuire and I met for three hours one night, and he offered me the job, and I said, "OK, let's do it." He told Sid at 10 o'clock at night. Sid's first question to McGuire was, "What does this mean for me?"

Sid was a great reporter, but one of his problems was that he wanted the truth to be what he wanted it to be. If the truth was negative toward his pals, he didn't want to report that.

I worked with Sid for 32 years at the *Star Tribune.* All the guys he loved, I didn't, and that was a problem between us.

I was admittedly too hard on Lou Holtz. But Bobby Knight was the biggest jerk that ever lived. And George Steinbrenner was a bully. And Billy Martin was just a weasel. Sid would have to walk a tightrope every time George fired and rehired Billy as Yankees manager because he loved both guys.

As I said, Sid was an unbelievable reporter. Back when I was the baseball beat writer, the drama every year at spring training was around who was going to make the team. We took the final roster much more seriously back then, and the angle of every story in spring training was, "This guy just went 2-for-3 and he's got a chance to be the fifth outfielder." We always figured the club had about seven job openings each season.

We would be writing these dramatic stories trying to predict who would make the final cuts. Then Sid would breeze in with about 10 days left in spring training, and the next day he would have the final 25-man roster. Every freaking year. We could never figure out how he got it because he and Calvin Griffith weren't tight. Years later, Tom Mee, the long-serving, feisty media relations director, told me, "I can't believe you guys never figured out where Sid got the roster every year." Then he said: "Ray Crump."

Ray Crump was the equipment manager. His wife sewed the names on the uniforms. Ray had to have the list of players 10 days before the season to get everything ready. Sid figured that out, and he'd get Crump to give him the list. We always blamed Howard Fox or Calvin, but it was Ray Crump.

Sid had those kinds of instincts. He had a great curiosity about what people did and figuring out who had the influence. He could walk into a room and know who the decision makers were.

The first five years of Joe's and my radio show were devoted to agitating Sid. An example: In 1991 Strike the Gold won the Kentucky Derby. I covered that derby because we had a horse with a Minnesota connection running.

Friday night before the race, I was there by myself at a hotel outside of Louisville. I found a little barbecue joint, almost out in the country. I was sitting there, and Dave Kindred and Hubert Mizell came in. They were veteran sportswriters who both had a relationship with Bobby Knight. They asked if they could join me, and I invited them to sit down. They said, "Knight's joining us with his wife. Is that OK?" I thought, *This will be interesting.* I had taken all these cheap shots at him over the years in my column.

The Knights came and sat down with us for dinner, and it was cordial. His wife was great. Finally, he turned and asked me how Sid was doing. I said, "Meaner than a snake." That was it.

The next day, Saturday morning, I called in to do the radio show. I started off the show by telling Sooch, "You know, every time I come to the Kentucky Derby, I like to have dinner the night before with Bobby Knight. Bobby comes all the time, and we like to get together before the race." I go on and on about this. Remember, this was first time I was at the derby. I knew Sid probably wasn't listening, but I was hoping it would get back to him.

Always a master of timing, Sooch said, "So, did Knight mention Sid at dinner?"

I said, "No, he really didn't. I got the impression that their whole relationship is overrated by Sid, that they're really not that close."

It was five minutes of satire. Apparently Sid started his radio show the next day with a tirade about how "Reusse doesn't even know Knight. He's never given him a chance."

Ninety-two percent of Sid's audience didn't listen to our show. They had no idea what the hell he was talking about. Dave Mona, his radio cohost, had no idea what he was talking about. But the moral of the story is: it worked.

Sid and I got along pretty good during the last 10, 12 years of his life. At some point, you just have to appreciate how amazing his life and career were. He was a physical marvel. His hearing went, and he broke a hip. Anybody else that age dies within a couple weeks after a breaking a hip. Sid was going to P. J. Fleck's press conference two weeks later.

Another part of Sid's genius was that he would send notes to people he had talked to for his column. Our office manager in the sports department, Terri Faris, wrote those notes before Sid signed them, and she kept hundreds of them over the years.

The notes always said either you're the greatest or you got screwed and you deserve better.

Sid knew there was no better way to an athlete's heart or a coach's heart than to tell them one of those two things. Sometimes it was, "You're the greatest and you got screwed."

Sid is No. 1 on my most unique list.

12

◆

TURKEYS: A THANKSGIVING TRADITION

For many Minnesotans, Thanksgiving starts with Reusse's annual "Turkey of the Year" column in the Star Tribune. *Those who cannot wait until the morning paper for the big reveal will stay up until the column posts online late the night before.*

What started as a column idea in a pinch has become an institution that inspires prop bets and family bonding.

■ ■ ■

While I was on the Twins beat for the *St. Paul Dispatch*, I was also writing a column on general sports subjects for the Thursday edition. For instance, I remember going to my first Kicks soccer game and writing that it had all the excitement of an 800-page James Michener novel, which didn't go over well with our soccer readers in the Twin Cities.

Back in the '70s, when I was still drinking, my brother and the whole Prior Lake crew would go to the bowling alley on the Wednesday night before Thanksgiving. There was no greater party night, even for us guys who were beyond college age. I didn't want to let my job interfere with that.

On the day before Thanksgiving in 1978, I was driving to the office at noon to write about something. There were a bunch of games in town that night, but I didn't want to write a column from

< 145 >

an event that started in the evening and required me to write on deadline for the next day's paper. I'm thinking and thinking. Somehow this occurs to me: *Turkeys. Thanksgiving. Turkeys. It would fit my personality to write about turkeys. I'll go in and think up 10 guys who are jerks and call it "Turkey of the Year."*

My first "Turkey of the Year" was Ohio State football coach Woody Hayes. The column got a little reaction on Thursday morning but nothing huge. Then, a month later, Hayes punched Clemson player Charlie Bauman at the '78 Gator Bowl, and I wrote something about how the Turkeys of the Year are predictive of behavior or something like that.

The next year I was writing columns full time. When Thanksgiving rolled around, I thought, *Well, this is a no-brainer. I'll do it again.*

The feature gathered momentum. The first five years, I was pretty gutless. Woody was the choice the first year because he was such a jerk. After that, I targeted guys Sid liked: Bobby Knight, George Steinbrenner, Pete Rozelle. They were all national figures.

The first year I went local was '83. I chose Paul Giel, the athletic director at the U of M. The day after I named him Turkey of the Year, Sid had a note in his column that Giel underwent open-heart surgery at the university hospital. I never prayed for a guy's recovery more in my freaking life.

In '84 it was Les Steckel, the embattled coach of the Vikings. That wasn't real tough. Lou Holtz was '85. On the Wednesday before Thanksgiving, the story broke that he was leaving Minnesota. My Turkey of the Year piece ran on Thursday, and on Friday it was announced that Holtz was going to Notre Dame. So that was a good choice too.

Every year I would get letters from readers about the Turkey column. I'd get calls at the radio station. Some people thought it was horrible, and some people thought it was hilarious.

I really made it hard work for myself a lot of years. I remember one year the theme was recipes that had turkey as a main ingredient. That took me like two days. My wife had a big cookbook, and I went through all these turkey recipes and tried to tie them in.

Lou Nanne didn't feel honored when I tagged him as Turkey of the Year for '88. I always got along with Louie. When I talked to him about it, he didn't laugh. I could see that it bothered him. That was the first year after I had moved to the *Star Tribune.*

I gave it to Kent Hrbek in 1990, and he also did not like it at all. The next time I ran into him after the piece was published, he announced that he was not going to talk to me for a year. But hey, Herbie was outstanding for a World Series–winning team the next year, so maybe the Turkey played its secondary role: motivation.

In 1996 I gave it to Olympic gymnast Kerri Strug for overplaying her injury at the Atlanta games. That one didn't go over too well with readers.

When I could figure out a way to not make the winner obvious, that was the best. But sometimes I had to go with the obvious choice.

One of my favorites was when I wrote the article to make it sound like Gophers football coach Tim Brewster was going to get Turkey of the Year (2007), and instead I gave it to Charlie Weis from Notre Dame. That was hard to write. My wife and I were in Phoenix on a little vacation. I spent two hours trying to make it read so that everybody would think, *I knew it was going to be Brewster,* only to get the curveball at the end.

University of Minnesota president Dr. Kenneth Keller got it in '86. He was an anti-sports guy, and he also got caught spending huge amounts of money to remodel his home. I was after him because he was de-emphasizing sports at the university.

The next year it was Carl Pohlad. I named him after the Twins won the World Series because he was the most boring speaker in the history of humankind. He would get up at parades and just make a dolt of himself. He couldn't speak in public. I thought I'd throw the ultimate curveball by giving it to him after his team won the world championship.

Pohlad is the only person to get it twice. He was Turkey of the Year again in 1998 for being so cheap.

A few years later, at spring training Sid said to me, "Hey, you should go write a column about Pohlad's mother."

I said, "Pohlad's mother? What do you mean Pohlad's mother?" Carl himself was like 80-something at the time, and I couldn't fathom that he had a living mother.

Sid said, "Yeah, she's right there. Her name is Mary."

So I went over and introduced myself to Mary Pohlad. Then I asked her, "Now, how old are you ma'am?" She said, "I'm 98." Then the guy who was there helping her pointed his thumb upward, indicating that she was even older.

Mary said, "What paper are you from?"

I replied, "The *Star Tribune.*"

She said, "Oh, that's my favorite paper. I've gotten that paper my whole life. There's that one guy there who keeps calling my son cheap. But I love that paper despite that guy."

So I told her, "Mary, when I get back to Minneapolis, we're going to track that guy down and get rid of him."

After the internet came along, the Turkey column only got bigger and bigger. I was intent on killing the column three or four years ago. But now, I don't know. It never died.

The column had a more humorous tinge to it the first 25 years or so, and I wish I could recapture that. The jokes are harder to come by, and to have a joke for everybody just became too hard. There was a period where the column got a little nastier than I wanted. I intended it to just be a little needling.

My two all-time highlights of Turkey of Year were in 1989 and 2015. After I named Mike Lynn the Turkey of 1989, he called me up on Thanksgiving morning and said, "It's about time. I've been waiting for this. What took so long?" I loved the guy because he got it.

And when Death was named the winner in 2015, the reaction was something else. A woman emailed me and shared that her family had a tradition that every year their father would read my column dramatically in the car as they drove to grandma's house on Thanksgiving Day. He had died earlier that year. So this year, the son, whose voice sounded like the dad's, read the article. When they got to the punch line—that the Turkey of the Year was Death—they had to pull over to the side of the road because they were all weeping. They couldn't believe it. Their story about what the Turkey column meant to them as an annual family tradition really touched me.

I wasn't entirely sure about the death angle. Flip Saunders had died that year, and there were several others, so death was on my mind. Before submitting the article, I called Dan Barreiro and asked what he thought. I ran it past a couple of other guys and told them to tell me the truth if they thought I shouldn't do it. They all said, *Go for it.*

There were times it took six, seven, eight hours to write the article. I always try to make each graph work together for a big setup at the end. Sometimes people get mad.

The great thing about the Turkey is—I figured this out with Hrbek in '90—you can call them out and either they continue to fail or the article motivates them. In 2018 I named P. J. Fleck the Turkey on Thursday, and then his team beat Wisconsin on Saturday. That was the point! We want to inspire. Whether they follow up with a failure or a victory, the Turkeys are undefeated!

Looking back, there are a few Turkeys I have some regrets about. Clem Haskins is one. If I had it to do over again, I wouldn't have given in to the pressure to name Clem the Turkey because of the academic scandal in '99.

Maybe Chris Doleman too. I was too hard on Doleman. I always thought he was an underachiever with the Vikings, and I named him the Turkey of 1991. Then he ends up in the Pro Football Hall of Fame.

13

CONFIRMED HACKER

On summer days when he wasn't at a baseball stadium, Reusse usually could be found on a golf course. He loved to play golf, though he never did it very well. And he loved to write about golf, which he does quite well.

Reusse was there to chronicle many iconic golf moments, from Tiger Woods's supernova arrival to Greg Norman's cringe-worthy choke at the Masters. Reusse's own playing days ended with an "oops" moment at a charity event.

■ ■ ■

I really do believe in the theory that "the smaller the ball, the better the writing." Golf and baseball fall into this category, and another thing they have in common is pace. The great advantage in golf writing is that the venue is as big a part of the story as the golfers. Football and soccer are played on the same sized field. You have variations in baseball, of course, but not like in golf. In golf everything is different. It allows for very descriptive writing, which I love.

I was never a great golfer myself. I had a big ol' left-to-right slice. I would aim north to go south. My playing was never worth a damn, but I got real passionate about it in the '70s and '80s. I

< 151 >

played a lot. I would play 50-something times during the summer. Every day off, I would play.

Going out for a few rounds of golf was a social event for the guys on the St. Paul sportswriting staff. We had a pretty good in with the club pros back then, these old guys at the prestigious golf courses. At North Oaks, Ray Vennewitz would say, "Come on up, boys." We could get in to these high-end courses, but we'd also play the easiest, cheapest courses we could find. It was mostly just a chance for all the buddies to get together. That's what we did on our days off. The fact that I never got any better really didn't hurt my pride too much.

The idea for the "Confirmed Hacker" series came when there was a lull with covering the Twins. I was always looking for things to write about in the summers when they stunk, and the "Confirmed Hacker" basically was invented as a one-off summer series to fill that gap. Plus, it was a great way to write about small-town Minnesota and do a little golfing.

This was how it worked: I would call up a golf course in Lanesboro or some place and say, "Hey, I'm going to be there on Tuesday, and I want to play with the four biggest screwballs you've got at the club. Get me the town characters." I always had a passion for being on the golf course with interesting characters.

I think the second one I did was at New York Mills, which was a homemade golf course in a sheep pasture. Some of the greens were fenced off so the sheep couldn't get in. It was like a five-stroke penalty for not closing the gate.

There was also an incredible bunch of characters at this course. I never will forget the owner introducing me to a guy named Delbert Sandbeck. He said, "Delbert is a good fella, but he hasn't talked much since he got hit in the head with a shot put in high school." I thought, *Alright, this one's going to work.*

The "Confirmed Hacker" feature went on for five or six years. I would do a series of five columns in one week. It was a lot of work because there always had to be a joke or a theme to it.

I got a tremendous reaction to the series. People sent me letters saying they loved it. The letters and messages I received about "Confirmed Hacker" were much more positive than, say, those about my coverage of Gophers football in the same time period. Every once in a while, I still get somebody asking me to bring back the "Confirmed Hacker."

At the end, though—along with it being a big space commitment for the paper—I was getting the mayor of the towns and the club presidents wanting to play. They were trying to use it as a PR opportunity for the community, rather than fulfilling the column's original intent, which was for the jokes, bringing together the funniest guys with the great one-liners.

When I had to come up with a name for the series, I wasn't sure what to call it. Then an idea hit me: "Confirmed Hacker." The name caught on with people. The paper also had a cartoon that ran with the feature. I was already full-figured then, and that cartoon made it look like some giant bubble boy was playing.

As I said, I was a hacker myself, with a nasty slice. I used to throw clubs in frustration like every other idiot who starts off playing golf with a god-awful swing and no idea what they're doing, thinking that somehow they're going to be good. I finally decided, *OK, from now on, I'm going to throw clubs when I hit a good shot.*

I played at some historic golf courses around the country over the years. I was willing to play anywhere, no matter how embarrassing it would be for me and those around me. I played Pinehurst No. 2, in North Carolina, twice. Uff da, that was hard.

One of my best golf memories was when I covered the 2002 British Open and then spent a few days afterward playing the course there. That was one of my favorite assignments ever. The Open was played at Muirfield, in a great little town just east of Edinburgh in Scotland. My good friend Mark Whicker and his wife, Robyn, and my wife, Katy, and I stayed in a little house that had a name on it—St. Matthews House—less than a mile from the golf course. Sooch also flew over, and we stayed after the Open and played five golf courses in two and a half days. It was fantastic. Every little town around there has a great golf course. One of my favorites was Dunbar on the Firth of Forth. You walk straight out toward the sea for half the course, then turn around and come back to the tiny, ancient clubhouse. And the weather might change four or five times in the process.

Over there you walked the course too. No carts. I remember wishing I could have a gin and tonic after a few days hauling my fat arse around those hills. But that's the passion I had for golf.

My playing days ended unceremoniously in 2004. I was playing in the 3M Open media event in Blaine. They would bring in the defending champ of the PGA's 3M tournament, and all the media guys would get to play free golf. I was in a group with the head of 3M and some other dignitary. And then Wayne Levi, who was the defending champ.

We got to hole No. 16, which had an elevated green, with a little valley in front. I was probably hitting my fourth shot in front of the green. I was going to try to hit a little flop shot to get it up there. The other three guys in my group were standing on the back of the green, probably figuring, *What damage can he do from 20 yards away?* Well, I bladed it perfectly and hit a screaming liner across the green. Levi jumped in the air and the ball hit him right on the knob of the ankle, and down he went.

Hollis Cavner, who runs the 3M tournament, started calling me the "Crippler." I was scared to death that Levi wasn't going to be able to play his next event that week. He played on Long Island and finished second. So I thought, *He'll be OK.* I went to see him when he was back in town for the 3M tournament. He was on the putting green, and he was not interested in having a conversation with me. He was a serious guy anyway. He wanted nothing to do with someone who darn near crippled him, and I can't say I blame him. That was the motivation to start weaning myself off the game of golf.

■ ■ ■

Loel Schrader came in as the sports editor at the St. Paul paper in the early '80s and wanted us to cover national events to raise our profile. He sent me to the Masters at Augusta National Golf Club in Georgia for the first time in '82. I went 18 times in 20-some years after that. I discovered that I love covering golf. I covered that British Open in '04 and the US Open seven or eight times, as well as some PGA Championships and Ryder Cups.

The 1991 US Open at Hazeltine changed golf in Minnesota. In 1970 the guy who finished second at the Open at Hazeltine, Dave Hill, said they ruined a good farm by punching 18 holes in it. The course was terrible. It was a terrible layout, and it was a pasture. The trees hadn't grown up yet. There were about eight trees out there.

The course opened in '62, and the US Women's Open was there in '66. The women were too nice to tell them it was a terrible golf course, but the men hated it and didn't hide it.

No. 16 originally was a par three where you'd hit the ball over a tree and down into a peninsula. P. J. Boatwright, the executive director of rules and competitions for the US Golf Association, told Hazeltine, "You'll never have an Open as long as that's your 16th hole."

Reed Mackenzie, later the USGA president, led an expedition along Lake Hazeltine to find the land to create a new 16th hole. They found room for a tee down in the weeds and built a new par four 16th that became the course's signature hole. This also gave them room to build a classic par three as No. 17.

They made other significant changes to the course as well. When the US Open came back in 1991, it was a triumph. The competitors praised the new golf course, and 40,000 people showed up to watch.

We had lightning the first day, and poor Billy Fadell, a spectator, lost his life. That was a real tragedy. But Minnesota fans came out in force that week, and it proved that we were crazy about golf.

The annual trips to Augusta for the Masters greatly improved my knowledge when it came to covering big-time golf. I got to know many prominent members of the golf media and learned a lot about the players and their quirks. It was an annual drama that I looked forward to as much as anything in my sportswriting career.

In '94 Tom Lehman, from Alexandria, Minnesota, had a chance to win at Augusta. He was leading going into the last day. José María Olazábal beat him. Tom spoke at a church there on Sunday morning before he went to the course. I went to the church to hear him and was all ready for him to win it. Then he got beat. I rode Tom's back pretty hard there for a few years.

Lehman's first Ryder Cup was in '97 at the Valderrama Golf Club in Spain. Somehow I convinced the editors to send me to cover our local boy. It was also Tiger Woods's first Ryder Cup. Earlier that year, Tiger had won the Masters by 12 strokes, and his impact on the sport was already being felt. Valderrama had a long par five at the top of a hill, and in the middle of the fairway, like 290 to 310 yards from the tee, they grew six inches of rough. Tiger was the only guy who was hitting drives 300 yards. I've seen other golf courses Tiger-proofed, but Seve Ballesteros, the captain of the European team, had them grow 20 yards of high grass in the middle of the fairway so Tiger would have to lay back just like everybody else.

A great part of covering the Masters was the newspaper characters I got to meet, the old southern golf writers. These were great guys who knew everybody. One year we were all hacking away on our advance columns on the Wednesday before the tournament. About three o'clock in the afternoon, the great Bill Millsaps from the *Richmond Times-Dispatch* got up to leave. I said, "I've still got two stories left to write, Billy. How are you finished?" He said to me with all his southern charm, "It's amazing how fast you can get done when you have no pride." What a beauty.

P. Dan Yates ran the interview room at Augusta National. He was the kid brother of Charlie Yates, who was a Ryder Cup golfer and great player and a big shot at the club.

P. Dan was quite the moderator. When golfers came in to the media room for interviews after a round, P. Dan would say, "We have such-and-such with us. Do you guys want him to go through birdies and bogeys, or do you want shot by shot?"

We'd say, "Birdies and bogeys."

And P. Dan would say, "Can you give us shot by shot?"

The media was treated very well at Augusta too. You'd think the Masters officials would be really arrogant and stuffy, but they weren't. A woman stationed at the entrance of the media room would always say in her deep southern drawl, "Well, hello, Mr. Reusse. How's things in Minnesota? Did you have a long winter?"

I loved it, man. I loved covering the Masters.

Greg Norman's collapse there in '96 was incredible. Norman played his first Masters in '81 and finished second twice during the '80s, but he had never won it all. Then, in '96, he had a six-shot lead heading into the final round, and it seemed like he was finally going to win his first green jacket. Then he went out on Sunday and shot 78 while Nick Faldo shot 67. He ended up losing by five strokes. You could just see how tormented he was. I'll give him credit now—even though I ripped him at the time—because Norman came in and spent 45 minutes in the pressroom right after his historic collapse. He just poured his heart out.

That's one thing about golf: there is no sport where you're more on an island by yourself. In no other individual sport is there such a slow and gradual process of choking. There's no other sport where it's so obvious that it's gotten to you.

One of the best things about covering golf is walking the courses and getting to hear great conversations. I was at the Masters one year when Ian Baker-Finch was on the tour. He had won the British Open in '91, and then suddenly he couldn't hit the ball straight, just started always hitting it left. The 13th hole at Augusta has a big tree line on the left from the tee box. It's basically a forest. I was there one day and about eight people were tromping through the forest. A spectator asked one of the old-time southern guys who worked security what was going on. The guy said, "They're looking for Ian Baker-Finch's ball. He's a danger to wildlife."

I was at Winged Foot when Fuzzy Zoeller beat Norman at the

'84 Open. That was the first time I encountered a New York golf crowd, which happened to include a bunch of drunk college students. This was when those fluorescent yellow balls were being used, and Hale Irwin and some other guys were playing a yellow ball. These college kids started following him around, chanting, "Play white balls. Play white balls." Hale blew up. They got to him. Every time you went to New York, it was great.

I was at Bethpage in Long Island when Tiger won the US Open in 2002. The crowd loved Tiger, but that was a New York crowd, man. Bethpage had a huge beer garden, and tons of fans were there drinking. Sergio Garcia was playing the Open, and he was dating tennis player Martina Hingis at the time. Fans started yelling at him that so-and-so was better looking than Martina. He also had the waggles. He'd adjust his grip constantly and fidget with the club over and over before his swing. Well, fans started counting the waggles. He couldn't pull the trigger. Then they'd yell at poor Colin Montgomerie: "Hey, Monty. Nice breasts." Oh god, they were brutal. That was the most raucous crowd of all time.

The best US Open I've ever covered was Pebble Beach in 2000. Tiger's performance there is the greatest sporting performance I have ever seen. He won by 15 shots. He was 12 under when nobody else was under par. It was unbelievable. He was hitting it from places that nobody else was hitting it from.

When Tiger had his fall from grace following accusations of infidelity in late 2009, everybody was shocked that he had succumbed to temptation. Really? As Chris Rock said, men are as faithful as their options, and Tiger had options. He was a young, good-looking, swashbuckling superstar.

Having covered sports for 50-plus years, I've always felt that we should judge our athletes as athletes. Now, if they're really bad guys beating somebody up and doing horrible things like that, that's an entirely different matter, but otherwise, I never concerned myself with whether they adhered faithfully to their wedding vows. I never let things like that change my opinion of somebody.

For a while, Tiger was winning in golf 40 percent of the time. In golf! This is a sport where the fewest number of people you're playing against is 90. It's an achievement that will never be approached again. The fact of the matter is, when he played really poorly, he still finished fourth. I've never seen anybody like Tiger Woods.

I also always appreciated that Tiger did his duty with the media. He wouldn't tell you a lot, but the demands on him from the media were unbelievable. We'll never see his like again.

14

◆

ASSIGNMENTS THAT STAND
FOR A LIFETIME

A writing career that spans more than five decades pushes the by-line count into the thousands. Reusse has written and witnessed a lot while covering sporting events around the globe.

Some columns are easy to forget as time passes, but there are assignments that stick with a writer forever. Reusse has enjoyed more than a few of those memorable occasions.

■ ■ ■

I was there for the World Series earthquake in 1989 in San Francisco. We had been to the Oakland Coliseum for the first two games. The A's had outclassed the Giants. This was the Giants' first time in the series since '62, and they were down 2–0 coming home.

It was a gorgeous day out there for Game 3. I was in the auxiliary press box, which was on the third level behind home plate. Tom Powers from the St. Paul paper was sitting next to me.

All of a sudden, we felt a shaking motion. Powers said, "What the hell is that?"

There was a jumbo jet right above us at that moment. I pointed up at the plane. About three seconds later he said, "That isn't a plane." We were rocking back and forth. The stadium was rattling.

I did not look up, but people said the light towers in the stadium were swaying. I was looking at the field, trying to figure out what was happening. It shook, shook, shook, shook. And then everything rumbled to a stop. Apparently it lasted only 18 seconds or something, but it seemed like 12 minutes.

The California crowd let out a big cheer when it stopped, like, *Wasn't that fun? It was just a little earthquake.*

Somebody noticed that some lights were out. Then the scoreboard went out, and everything else went out. I thought, *Well, it's going to take a while to get the electricity back.*

We still thought they were going to play the game. There were little TVs on press row that continued working. They showed that a portion of the Bay Bridge had collapsed. Then they showed the fire in the Marina District.

It soon became obvious that they were not going to play the game. The phones and power had gone out in the press box, but there was a little workroom on the level below us. Guys started going in there to write.

About 45 minutes after the earthquake, I was in that workroom, and we were told to evacuate the stadium. I went downstairs, and it was just starting to get dark. ABC news had a bunch of trucks and equipment outside the stadium, and they had lights running off a generator.

We didn't have cell phones or laptop computers back then. We had these Radio Shack word processors. I had batteries in my Radio Shack, and I stood there outside, using ABC's lights, and typed up 25 inches describing what I experienced.

There was a pay phone out there that was still working, but 15 reporters were lined up to use it. They were calling their newsrooms and dictating stories. It was going to be an hour and a half before I could use that phone.

I said the hell with it, and I hauled my large frame back up to the auxiliary press box. It was dark by then, and three or four guys were in there, and I could just make out their shadows. They were in there typing, and nobody was yelling for them to get out.

I started picking up telephones to see if any of them were alive.

I finally got one that was working, so I hooked it up to my Radio Shack word processor and sent in my column. It appeared to go through, but when I hung up the phone and tried to call back to see if they received the transmission in Minneapolis, the phone was dead. I could not find another working phone up there.

I went back downstairs, and we could see that traffic was just ungodly going back into the city. The media hotel was downtown. I was staying at the Embassy Suites out by the airport. One of the few smart things I ever did in my life.

I had a rental car, and it took me about an hour just to get out of the parking lot. I still didn't know whether the paper received my story or not. I drove back to the Embassy Suites, and the power was out there too. I had to walk up eight flights in the dark. I got in my room, and there was no power.

I went to bed, and at about three in the morning the whole place started rumbling again. The aftershock was more frightening than the earthquake.

That morning, I went to a gas station and found a pay phone. I called the *Star Tribune* office and asked, "Did that thing I sent last night make it?" They said, "Yeah, it's in the paper. And they've been trying to find you because they want you to drive over to Oakland today." That's where the freeway had collapsed.

I knew the Bay Bridge was closed and there would be no way for me to get to the Golden Gate. So I decided to drive south and try to get across to the east bay on the Dumbarton Bridge, even though I had never been on that bridge before.

As I was driving across the Dumbarton, I heard on the radio that they were going to be closing the bridge in 15 minutes. I got across and turned north and got to where the Bay Bridge had collapsed. There were people all over, and I could see the cars still up on the bridge; some of them were smushed.

All these guys who were hanging around there were presenting themselves as heroes. They were telling stories about saving lives and pulling people from rubble, but it wasn't true. It was just fantasized heroics for these young fellows.

A guy came out of a little tenement-type house nearby. I asked if he had been there last night, and he said, "Yeah." I asked his name, but he wouldn't tell me.

Apparently, he was busy with his Oakland lady friend, who was not the missus. He was a crew member on a freight ship and was in port, you know. But he told me he heard the cries from the bridge and he could hear people yelling for help. He was the one guy I trusted to quote because he didn't want anybody to know who he was, so I knew he wasn't just seeking attention.

I wrote my story and then flew home that night because the *Star Tribune* was sending three news reporters to cover the earthquake. I was back in San Francisco a week later for the end of the series. I know some people were saying they should call it off and not play. But it was kind of like after 9/11—it was therapeutic to play.

For about a month afterward, I would take false steps. Every once in a while, I would take a step and feel like the ground wasn't there. It makes no sense.

Right after the earthquake happened, I called my wife, Katy. She was home and had a couple of her girlfriends over. I said, "Dear, I just wanted to tell that it's been nice. I love you. Hopefully I'll see you again."

When we hung up, she said to her friends, "I wonder what that was about."

They turned on the TV and saw there had been an earthquake.

One of my favorite stories from that event involved my dear friend Carl Peterson from the St. Paul paper, one of the crotchety slot editors on the desk. Great newspaper guy, but someone who was very worried about his image as a well-dressed, polite gentleman.

He and his wife, Judy, were in the Marina District in San Francisco when the earthquake hit. They were walking near a Kentucky Fried Chicken that had one of those big buckets on a pole. The bucket was swaying in their direction. I always said that Carl's fear wasn't so much death as it was the humiliation of death by a chicken bucket. All around the nation he would be remembered in newspaper clippings as "Carl Peterson, 48, Killed by a Kentucky Fried Chicken Bucket."

■ ■ ■

Auto racing, specifically stock car racing, became phenomenally popular in this country for a time in the late 1980s and into the '90s. I had been to a couple of Daytona 500 races. I went to Richard Petty's last 500. Mark Whicker from the *Orange County Register* and I got an interview with Richard in his trailer, and he accused me of being a communist because I was from Minnesota, which was hilarious.

I also covered the Daytona 500 in 2001. It was a good race. Michael Waltrip and Dale Earnhardt Jr. battled down the stretch. When Dale Earnhardt Sr. hit the wall on the final lap, it looked harmless enough, except the car didn't go anywhere. The front end kind of stuck to the wall.

I was in the press box next to my friend Lenox Rawlings, a columnist from Winston-Salem, North Carolina. He was much more of a veteran auto racing guy than I was from living down there in NASCAR country. We decided to just listen to the interviews that were broadcast in the press box instead of walking 20 minutes down the track to get to the interview room.

After the race, one of the drivers was being interviewed on the TV. The reporter asked, "And how is Dale doing?" The driver said, "Somebody else is going to have to answer that."

Lenox looked at me and said, "We better get down there."

By the time we got to the interview room, the gate to the garages was closed. Usually, you could just walk in and wander around the garages when the race was over. We couldn't get in this time.

Then we saw Earnhardt family members heading to Dale Sr.'s trailer, and they were weeping. We didn't quite get what was happening. Everyone thought it was just another accident.

Then Dave Ferroni, a Minnesota friend and PR guy in the racing business, walked over to Lenox and me and said, "He's dead." The official announcement came about an hour later.

That's the last race I ever went to. Not because I was traumatized by seeing death; it just worked out that way. But man, Dale Sr. was popular. People loved him.

That day reinforced for me that when you go to cover a sporting event, you've got to be prepared for anything.

■ ■ ■

As part of sports editor Loel Schrader's efforts to get the *Pioneer Press* and *Dispatch* to cover more national stories, he sent me to Alabama to talk to Bear Bryant, the legendary football coach. This was 1980 or '81, back when the teams took a week off before the Iron Bowl, the great 'Bama–Auburn rivalry game. I called the sports information director at Alabama and told him I'd like to come down and interview Bryant. The director called back and said, "Coach said he can do it Saturday morning."

I showed up at the football office at 9:30 that morning. Nobody was around. I went to Bryant's office and knocked on the door. He was in there, and we started b.s.-ing.

Then a couple of his turkey hunting buddies showed up, and they started telling stories. I was just sitting off to the side, writing in my notebook as fast as I could.

I mean, several books had been written about Bear Bryant by this time. They didn't need me to tell how many games he'd won and stuff like that. This was what I wanted: turkey hunting stories with his friends.

It was a fun morning, just listening to Bryant and his buddies tell tales. I was in there for probably 90 minutes. Every once in a while, Bear would turn to me and say, "Anything else you want there, son?"

The experience changed my opinion of Bryant completely. I had thought he was this grumpy old son of a gun, but he was a hell of a guy. Even his buddies had a reverence for him—they all called him "Coach"—but he was as happy to see his friends as they were to see him. They would tell a Bear story, and he'd get a big grin on his face.

I also was at Bear's last game as coach. It was the '82 Liberty Bowl, when 'Bama beat Illinois, 21–15.

My meeting with Bryant reminds me of another encounter I had with an all-time football icon and the time I got to spend a few hours with George Halas.

When I was a kid in Fulda, before the Vikings came to Minnesota, our team was the Bears. Sioux Falls TV would carry the Bears games on Sundays. "Papa Bear" George Halas and the Bears. He had the look of a very surly gentleman.

Fast-forward to years after he's done coaching and running the team as owner. He had a little office in Chicago on State Street, working with his old ticket manager, and they were selling tickets to a handful of old-time Bears fans. They had about 25 customers who still went to George to get their tickets, guys who had been buying from him since 1942 or something.

I arranged to see George on a Friday morning. I had been in California, so I took a red-eye from Los Angeles and landed at six in the morning. I went to see him and spent two hours with him. Nicest guy that ever lived. It was unbelievable. He showed me around his office. He had all these great pictures on the wall and memorabilia.

I flew back home and wrote a 100-inch story on Saturday morning and could have written much more because Halas was so good.

■ ■ ■

When We Were Kings is the greatest documentary in the history of man. Unbelievable. Hilarious. The fight between Muhammad Ali and George Foreman was in '74, and the documentary came out in '96.

I went to an afternoon showing at the Lagoon theater in Minneapolis, and when I got home, I told Katy, "I've gotten a chance to talk to damn near everybody that I want to in sports, but never in a small group with Ali."

I had been at a couple of his press conferences over the years, but there were a hundred people there, and I didn't get to ask any questions. Never had a chance to really meet Muhammad Ali.

An hour after I got back from watching the documentary, the phone rang, and it was Harvey Mackay, the successful local businessman who became a best-selling author. Harvey said, "Patrick, I've got a book signing tomorrow. Would you like to spend a half hour with Muhammad Ali?" Harvey was paying Muhammad to come in for the book signing.

I said, "You're damn right I would."

He told me to come to the Radisson Hotel, room such-and-such. Be there at 10:30 in the morning.

I showed up and Hondo the magician was there doing card tricks. Ali had Parkinson's disease at this point, but he was doing fine. He had an assistant there. And Harvey was there.

I wasn't really interviewing Ali; I was just listening to the conversations and chatter. I stayed there for a half hour hearing a few stories from him. And he loved the magic tricks.

Sid came by too. Harvey said, "Muhammad, this is Sid Hartman from the paper, a local legend."

Ali said, "Sid Hartman? Sid Hartman?!"

He stood up and clenched his fist and said, "Sid Hartman, Sid Hartman. You're the guy who called me a . . ." Let's leave it at that.

Sid started backing up, saying, "No, no, no, no, no. I would never do that."

Apparently, this was one of Muhammad's go-to tricks. He had Sid scared to death. I'm glad he pulled it on Sid and not me.

That day was a thrill of a lifetime, to see how engaging and charismatic Muhammad was up close and in person.

■ ■ ■

For the Olympics, the *Star Tribune* would send writers out across the country to do advance stories. In 1992, before Barcelona, I went to California. First I went to northern California to cover the finals of the Greco-Roman trials, because Minnesota was going to have wrestlers on the Olympic team. One was silver-medalist-to-be Dennis Koslowski.

Then I took a flier and went to southern California in the hopes of seeing Oscar De La Hoya, the great young boxer. He was still a teenager, 19 years old. The box-off for all weight classes had not yet been held, but it was very likely that Oscar was going to be on the Olympic team.

I got ahold of Oscar's cousin, who was handling his PR. His cousin said, "Yeah, come on out."

I went to their house in East Los Angeles. I met Oscar and his father, Joel, who was a great guy. His mother had died, and they had a shrine to her in the house.

I went and watched Oscar work out at this old gym where he trained. I talked to him probably for an hour, and I talked to everybody else in his close circle. I was hanging out in their living room, and we went to dinner that night. I got to know Oscar and the family a little bit.

They told me he would be sparring the next day with Shane Mosley, and if I wanted to stick around, I could watch. Answer: Definitely.

The sparring session was held at the Resurrection Gym, which was in an abandoned Catholic church. I watched Oscar spar five or six rounds with Mosley, who had been upset in the Olympic trials and didn't even make the box-off.

In Barcelona, I was rooting for Oscar every match, and he made it to the finals. I went over and stood with his dad and a couple other family members when he was boxing for and winning the gold medal.

That worked out pretty damn well, I'd say.

■ ■ ■

Before the women's basketball Final Four in Minneapolis in 1995, I went to North Carolina to do a story because the Tar Heels were the defending national champs. I wrote about their point guard, Marion Jones, who got in the news later for something less than flattering (performance-enhancing drugs). I then went to UConn for a couple of days, and then I went to Tennessee on the promise that I could talk to the great coach Pat Summitt. Her PR person couldn't give me an exact time for the interview, but I went down to Knoxville anyway.

It was a game day for the Tennessee Volunteers. I was introduced to Pat an hour or so before the game. Then the game ended, and she did her postgame press conference. I was getting nervous that my interview with her wasn't going to happen. The PR person told me not to worry, I'd get her.

About an hour after the game, I walked into a big room that led to an auxiliary gym. There were two chairs set up. It was 11 o'clock at night by this point, and Summitt gave me an hour interview. She was unbelievable.

I was as impressed with her knowledge, demeanor, and ability to articulate exactly what she wanted to tell you as anyone I've ever been around. It was just fantastic.

There is zero doubt in my mind that Pat Summitt could have coached men. She could stomp that right foot on the floor and give that stare, and everybody would pay attention.

She had the Bud Grant stare. That is really an asset. The number of people who can coach just by looking at you is very rare.

Being at Tennessee reminded me of one of my favorite college football games. No. 1 on that list was Nebraska–Miami at the '84 Orange Bowl, but top five, for sure, was when Raghib "Rocket" Ismail and the Notre Dame Fighting Irish went to Tennessee in 1990. That was freaking unbelievable. I have never seen an atmosphere like that in my life. The Vol Navy was there in full force on the Tennessee River, 100,000 people were going crazy in Neyland Stadium, and the Rocket was as great as advertised on the field—it was just a hellacious environment.

We have college football here in Minnesota, and I was around for the glory years long ago. I certainly have seen the Gophers crowd jumping a few times: Glen Mason's team playing Michigan in '03 when they choked it away, and P. J. Fleck's squad when they won 11 games a few years ago. But you go to the South for a big game like that, and it was a different animal.

Another game I loved was at Texas A&M after Jackie Sherrill became the first million-dollar college football coach. It was his first game as coach at A&M in September '82, and they were playing Boston College.

My old buddy Randy Galloway had just become a columnist in Dallas, and he picked me up at the airport. We drove to College Station and ate at a place called Tom's Barbecue on Friday night before the game. Jackie sat with us at dinner and basically told us how humble he was. There were about eight writers there.

Jackie told us great stories, and I was planning to write a column about how Jackie was going to turn A&M into a football power. Then Doug Flutie and Boston College kicked A&M all over the field, defeating them 38–16.

This was back when teams scheduled Boston College for a win. But Flutie came in and lit them up. Everyone was stunned. The whole atmosphere, with the bonfire on Friday night and the pomp, was great—except the team forgot to show up, and Doug Flutie killed them.

Another memorable college football moment came after poor John Gutekunst became the Gophers coach in 1986, after Lou Holtz left. His first road game was at Oklahoma. We went down to Norman, and it felt like 110 degrees. Back then, if you were sitting on one side of the stadium, you almost couldn't see the other sideline because that field was so crowned. When Oklahoma ran their wishbone offense, they were always running downhill.

Barry Switzer was the Oklahoma coach. On Friday, the day before the game, I got 45 minutes alone with Switzer in his office before practice. It was one of the most amazing interviews ever because I could tell he was thinking about something else but still gave a hell of an interview. He was very cordial and relaxed.

What I remember most about that interview was him telling me a story about recruiting a kid from Dallas. The kid's home was in a tough area. Switzer went down there with an assistant coach, and when they got to the home, Switzer told the assistant to drive around to the back first. He wanted to drive through the alley.

They went to the alley, and Switzer got out of the car and started looking through the family's garbage can. He saw eight empty Pearl beer bottles in there. They drove back around front and went inside the house. They started talking to the parents, and the kid's dad asked, "Barry, would you like a beer?"

Barry said, "Only if it's a Pearl."

That's how you recruit.

The other thing: Oklahoma edged poor Gutey and the Gophers 63–0 that day.

Doug Grow was at the game writing columns for Minneapolis, and I was writing them for St. Paul. A 20-year-old blond Oklahoma woman was standing there when the Gophers were walking up the runway to the locker room after the game. She said, "We sure enjoyed having you boys. You come back real soon."

Grow and I looked each other. I said, "I get that," and he said, "No, I get that."

It was the punch line in both columns.

College football is ripe with old-timey characters. For years, I had heard stories from my buddies in the South about Frank Howard, the legendary Clemson coach. Long after he retired, I got Howard on the phone before the Gophers were going to play Clemson in the Independence Bowl in December '85. Lou had just left. Gutey was coaching them in the bowl for his first game as head coach.

I called up Howard, and he said, "Where you from, boy?"

I said, "The *St. Paul Dispatch*."

Howard said, "The *St. Paul Dispatch*? Does that paper get out of the city limits?"

I told him I knew he was a fantastic coach at Clemson and went to a lot of bowl games and blah, blah, blah.

Then he asked, "What's your record up there?"

I said, "6–5."

He said, "Yeah, we're 6–5 too. You know, I went to the Orange Bowl and the Sugar Bowl and the Cotton Bowl. If you lost more than one game, you didn't go to any of those bowl games. This one ain't no bowl game. This is a battle of pissants."

15

A TO Z OF COLORFUL CHARACTERS

◆

Reusse loves unique characters, people he affectionately refers to as "all-timers" or "beauties"—the kind of personalities who can make you laugh, cringe, or shake your head about how they live their lives or excel at their professions. Characters provide stories that may be printable and others that are not suitable for print. Some of their stories might sound fictional, but as Reusse says, "That's too good not to be true." Reusse has encountered so many one-of-a-kind characters that he lists here some of his favorites, A to Z.

■ ■ ■

A: Mike Augustin. As close a friend as a guy can have. He rescued me from financial straits in Duluth by hiring me at the *St. Cloud Times*. Mike loved St. John's University. He was well-known for being what St. Thomas people call a "Johnny Lover." But when he got pancreatic cancer and died way too young at age 57, one of the guys in the room and holding his hand was his close friend Steve Fritz, the ultimate Tommie. That's the kind of guy Mike Augustin was.

B: Bobby Bell. My all-time favorite Gophers football player. I say he is the greatest Gopher of all time. He was such an athlete playing interior defensive tackle at about 230 pounds. He could not be blocked. He would have led Minnesota to three straight Rose

Bowls were it not for a questionable call by the refs in the Wisconsin game in 1962. And remember, the Vikings picked Bobby Bell in the NFL draft but didn't sign him because Kansas City of the AFL beat them to it. One reason the Vikings lost that Super Bowl in '69: Bobby Bell was one of the eight Pro Football Hall of Famers on that Kansas City Chiefs team.

C: Ron Coomer. Coom Dog, man. Bad years for the Twins were extra dreary when they were in the Metrodome, and the Coom Dog was all we had going for us from about '96 to '99. He was a standout in the dullest period in Twins history. To see Coom Dog surface as an extremely popular guy in his hometown of Chicago broadcasting Cubs games is just fantastic because we all love Coom Dog.

D: Joe Driscoll. I have encountered scores of characters attached to town team baseball, and I will put Driscoll up against any of them. He was a great three-sport athlete at Le Sueur High School and could have been outstanding at all three at Southwest State if it wasn't for those darn classes. Pitcher and hitter in baseball, shooter in basketball, quarterback and punter in football. He even had a pro football tryout as a punter. He was an all-time great town baller at Arlington, Red Wing, Dundas, back home at Le Sueur, and anyplace else that would have him. A few years ago, I was doing my radio show from the press box at an empty Fort Myers stadium. It was March 17, and I got a call from Driscoll complaining that Murphy's Bar in Kilkenny was closed on St. Patrick's Day. He asked me, "What are you going to do about it?" I replied, "I'm as offended as you are, Joe. But I'm 1,700 miles away, and I don't know if I can solve your problem."

E: Carl Eller. Carl is here to represent the Purple People Eaters. One of the great days of my journalistic life was when we were writing a "100 years of Minnesota sports" series for the *Star Tribune* in 1999, and I got to go with Carl and Jim Marshall to see Justice Alan

Page in his office. Here's the dignified Justice Page with his bow tie, and when these two guys walked in it was like an old-time locker room full of storytelling. Eller was also a great Gophers lineman when that team was very important to my mental well-being in the early '60s.

F: Jim Fregosi. He was one of those baseball characters I got to know. One time when he was managing the Angels, I ripped him in a column in the *Dispatch*, saying he had gotten out-managed in a game. Fregosi, who once proclaimed that he reads every comma, had somehow found this column. People in St. Paul hadn't even seen it. When the Angels were in Minnesota the following year, I got invited to dinner at Charlie's Café Exceptionale in downtown Minneapolis. Fregosi was hosting it with all his coaches, the media that covered the Angels, and me. He had a seat waiting for me right next to him. When the meal was done, he said, "Did you get enough to drink? Was the meal OK? Did you like the company?" I said, "Yeah, I enjoyed everything." Then he said, "Well, why are you such a jackass then?" From that moment on, he and I had a great relationship. When I heard he passed away in 2014 it was a sad day.

G: Mike Grant. He grew up with his dad, Bud, and played for and coached with John Gagliardi, probably the two greatest football coaches in Minnesota history. Mike has built a powerhouse high school program at Eden Prairie. I know people look at Eden Prairie's enrollment size as an unfair advantage, like it's a big football machine. But what I love about Mike is he took the best football lessons from both of those guys, his dad and Gagliardi, and applied them to his coaching. He also learned this from his old man: Go to the cabin.

H: Torii Hunter. When Torii came back to the Twins for that one-year swan song in 2015, we got to see his big personality more than ever. He was just a guy who enjoyed becoming a great baseball player. I don't think his name is mentioned often enough among the all-time great Twins. When naming the all-time Twins lineup, he's got to be the third outfielder. It's Tony Oliva and Kirby Puckett and Torii. Puckett has to go play left or something because Torii has to be the center fielder on that team.

I: Willard Ikola. Long before he created a hockey powerhouse at Edina as a coach, Ike was a fantastic goalie at Eveleth High. He led the team to three straight state championships. Some people don't know that about him. He was an Olympic goalie in '56 and played in world championships. In 1999, when we were doing that 100-year piece for the *Star Tribune*, I had Ike ride up to Eveleth with me. I spent a day with him, and the stories he told were wonderful. My favorite moment was sitting in the bar up there, having lunch. I said, "Ike, what happened to Eveleth hockey? How come they're not the powerhouse anymore?" He said, "See that guy at the end of the bar? Go ask him." I asked the guy to explain to me what happened to Eveleth hockey. The fella said, "They started marrying Virginia girls and screwed up the bloodlines."

J: Bobby Jackson. My all-time favorite Gophers basketball player. The team went to the Final Four in '97 for several reasons, but Jackson was the guy who took them there. Just an absolute warrior, and a good dude. He spent 12 years in the NBA as a player, and I'm glad to see him having success as an NBA assistant coach. He will probably be a head coach someday. I have a lot of favorite Gophers players, but he's No. 1 on the list.

K: Jim Kaat. I watched him pitch and admired him greatly. I admired the fact that after the Twins got rid of him because they thought his arm was dead, he pitched for another 12 years. I had him as a regular guest on my radio shows for four or five years. He can't be stumped. There's not a topic you can raise that he doesn't have two great stories about, minimum. He's in his early 80s now, and he's still as great as he's ever been as an announcer. I was so glad to see him finally get the recognition he deserved by being inducted into the National Baseball Hall of Fame in 2021.

L: Tom Lehman. I got to follow Tom around and walk the golf course with his dad, Jim, at Augusta National for the Masters Tournaments and at US Opens. I got to see Tom's moments of triumph (such as winning the British Open in 1996) and some heartbreaking losses—most notably at the '96 US Open at Oakland Hills, when he bogeyed the last hole and lost by one stroke, and at the Masters in '94, when he lost by two strokes to José María Olazábal. For five years he hit it closer to the hole than anybody else in golf, including Tiger Woods. He just wasn't a great putter. Otherwise, his very fine golf record would have been a great record. He moved to Arizona and has lived there for years, but Alexandria is still home for him. He's really a high-class guy.

M: Pat Micheletti. My all-time favorite Gophers hockey player. Micheletti was something back in the day. Great scorer, great sniper, great at stirring up trouble on the ice. He comes from a well-known hockey family in Hibbing. Pat is my go-to hockey guy. His older brother Jerry gave him a kidney that saved his life. The Michelettis are all great guys.

N: Pete Najarian. Pete is an all-timer. He was a really great football player on some really bad Gophers teams. He was on the field when Nebraska beat them 84–13 in '83, and I think he had 20-something tackles in that game. I had him as a radio guest quite frequently. To see Pete become a world-famous financial advisor is amazing. His dad, Dr. John, was a world-famous transplant surgeon. Pete has the same attitude as his dad. He's representative of a fantastic family.

O: Heidi Olhausen. She was the player who attracted me to watch Gophers volleyball. I had pretty much avoided the sport my whole career until the early '90s, when she and Kate Callahan came from Lakeville to play for the U. Heidi is another great character. She was my introduction to volleyball and the realization that, hey, this sport is fun.

P: Terry Porter. I'm not talking about the Timberwolves' Terry Porter, although he deserves mention too because he's a very classy guy. This is Terry Porter from Marshall, Minnesota. Greatest three-point shooter I ever saw. Unfortunately, they didn't have a three-point line when he played. He was a star on the 1963 Marshall team that beat Cloquet in what I consider the greatest high school basketball final ever in the one-class days. Then he went to St. Cloud State, and lo and behold, his last two years there I was covering him for the *Times*. We were about the same age. He could really shoot it.

Q: Frank Quilici. Frankie was my first manager as a Twins beat writer. He did a really good job considering how underfinanced the team was. My first year, '74, they should have been terrible, and they finished 82–80. He became an announcer later on, and I had a lot of fun with him during that time. He was happy in that role. Indirectly, he also helped Joe Soucheray and me with our radio careers because Greg Harrington doing his impersonation of Frank Quilici was one of the triggers that made *Monday Night Sports Talk* a success.

R: Tom Reid. He was kind of the Frank Quilici of the North Stars as a player-turned-broadcaster, though he never coached. He had a long career as a player and then as a broadcaster. People talk about him making his penalty shot against Canadiens Hall of Fame goalie Ken Dryden like it was the greatest thing in the history of hockey. Tom was a rugged defenseman who never looked to score, but he beat the great Dryden on that night in October 1971. People got a kick out of the stunned reaction. Lou Nanne has to settle for

1A in the contest of great hockey storytellers because Tom Reid is right there with him.

S: Flip Saunders. I go back to Flip playing for the Gophers from 1974 to '77 and being the plucky point guard. After he died in 2015 at the age of 60, my son Jim called as I was writing the obituary. Jim's eulogy to Flip was, "He was our point guard." That was it. Flip was our point guard. He was the definition of a point guard. When Flip showed up with the Gophers, we were like, *Oh, that's what a point guard is.* Of course, he had two runs with the Timberwolves as coach. The first was a good 10 years that saw the only success the team has ever had. He died way too young. It was a shock to all of us. One thing I loved are the stories about how he'd be up at three o'clock in the morning watching the Home Shopping Network and buying tons of crap. There was not a gadget he did not own. But he's a first-name celebrity here. Say "Flip" and you don't have to say anything more.

SSS: Triple S. Samantha Seliger-Swenson. When I really got on the Gophers volleyball bandwagon, Samantha was the setter. Watching her for four years (2015–18) gave me a better understanding of what they're trying to accomplish on the court. She was the best quarterback on campus. Before her, I thought volleyball was just the ball going over the net and back. Then I saw her play and thought, *OK, there's much more organization and strategy to this than I comprehended.* She's a great person too. I called her Triple S in my columns. She was very important to my volleyball growth.

T: Jerry Tarkanian. Before Loel Schrader became sports editor of the St. Paul paper, he was the columnist in Long Beach. He was pals with Tark when he was the coach at Long Beach State. Loel set me up to spend three, four hours with Tark one day, and man, what an experience. My favorite basketball game ever was when

Tark's UNLV team thrashed Duke in the '90 championship game. Then they lost to Duke the next year, which was heartbreaking because I'm not a Duke guy. But when they thrashed them that night in '90 and the game ended, the first guy who came down and hugged Tark was Sonny Vaccaro from Nike. I thought, *This is the way it should be!* Tark made no secret of the fact that college sports were big business and that shoe companies had tremendous influence. And his UNLV teams in the late '70s looked like five helicopters going up and down the court. It was run-and-gun. Tark gave us 15, 16 years of great basketball.

U: Bob Uecker. I got to meet Ueck through my friend Mike Gonring, who covered the Brewers for the *Milwaukee Journal.* Uecker is a natural, man. He could walk onto the Johnny Carson set and do a bit. It's amazing; he's still going in his 80s. He loves baseball so much and loves the broadcast booth so much that he's still working. During the COVID pandemic in 2020, I was trying to do a piece on him. The PR folks were going to have me do a video interview on Zoom. I was at the Milwaukee ballpark for the Twins game, and when Ueck saw that, he said, "Ah, come here." We sat and talked with our masks on for 25 minutes. He's just a good guy. In spring training years ago at Sun City, I was there with the Twins and went to see Ueck in the broadcast booth. He asked me if I wanted a beer. I said, "Nah, that's OK. I haven't been drinking lately." So he went back on the air and said, "We've had a lot of surprises this spring, but Patrick Reusse from the St. Paul newspaper just told me he quit drinking. That is a surprise." And he was right.

V: Jesse Ventura. Jesse, God love him. He and I did not part well, but I did two years of radio with him, and I loved it. I did two call-in segments with him each morning. They were a little tough because all he wanted to talk about was Champlin Park football—he was a volunteer assistant coach—and the Timberwolves and the Vikings. It's amazing to me that he made his money and his reputation having people scream the vilest insults at him, but he was the most thin-skinned guy in the world of politics. When the Timberwolves finally made the playoffs, they had him rappel down a rope onto the court before the game. I wrote that they wanted a guy who wouldn't get hurt if he fell and landed on his head. It was funny. Jesse didn't think it was funny. He's unique, and I'm glad I had those experiences with him, even though he's probably unhappy that he had them with me.

W: Earl Weaver. This covers a lot of territory, but I can say without question that Weaver is my all-time favorite opposing coach or manager facing a Minnesota team. He was one of those opposing managers who, if you became familiar to him at all, you could sit next to him in the dugout and talk for 30 minutes before a game. He was unique, man. When I went on the road with the Twins, he was the only guy I'd go visit before I went to the Twins clubhouse, just to see what he was up to. He used to be about the only manager who came to the Twins Room at the Metrodome to have some drinks. When he'd get rolling, he was the funniest guy ever. Everything you saw with his arguments with umpires and crazy antics on the field, that was him.

X: Joe Soucheray. Sooch is the X factor in my media career. God love him. He was the radio talent. He made radio a remarkable element of his working life, not a hobby like I did. As a team, he was Abbott and I was Costello. It was always "Joe and Pat," and that was the proper order. Joe proved his radio mettle when he created *Garage Logic* as KSTP-AM's daily staple starting in the mid-'90s. It became known as simply "GL" to a huge audience, and it was a mythical place of common sense that remains mighty in the podcast era. We still partnered on occasion, and the bottom line never changed: Joe's the talent, and I'm along for the ride.

Y: Dan Barreiro. Dan is the Y factor in my media career. He was ensconced as the *Star Tribune*'s essay-style sports columnist when I came in from St. Paul in June 1988 to be the second of those. We had been competitors; if we didn't mesh as colleagues, sportswriting could've gotten to be a lot less fun than it had been. Turned out, we split the important duties and became great friends. Then Dan went off and became a radio sensation with his *Bumper to Bumper* on KFAN, which became the dominant afternoon drive show on local radio. When I was at AM-1500 I was among those he buried in the ratings—and for good reason. Dan gets radio and remains driven to do it right.

Z: Fred Zamberletti. The best reason to drive to Mankato and go to Vikings training camp was to sidle up next to Zamby, their longtime trainer, and ask him what was happening. Even if I was on the outs with the Vikings over something I had written, I was always in with Zamby. He knew I was an OK guy in my heart. Zamby once called me because I had taken a shot at Anthony Carter in my column about something. He said, "Patrick, you're wrong about that one." That was the only time he did that. I took it to heart: *OK, I was wrong. I'm not taking any more shots at Anthony Carter.* I went to see Zamby when he was dying and spent a couple of hours in his hospital room. He was pretty out of it, but he could look at me, and he knew I was there. Of all the people I dealt with at the Vikings, Zamby was my No. 1 guy.

EPILOGUE

Given the might with which Minnesotans fought against public financing for stadiums and arenas for the first 40 years as a major league location, the phenomenon of the twenty-first century is the avalanche of gifts we've provided to our sports teams over the last two decades.

Met Stadium, a wonderful erector set for which citizens bought bonds in the mid-1950s, served as home to both the Twins and the Vikings from 1961 to 1981. After a fierce battle with the grassroots "Save the Met" insurgents, Max Winter and Sid Hartman gained the Metrodome—built so cheaply that it originally didn't come with air conditioning. The quirky place did account for an 8–0 record in two World Series, so our original Dome always will have that going for it.

As for our original NHL arena, Met Center, it was as wonderful in its own low-budget way as was the ballpark across the parking lot in Bloomington. It also was slapped up in less than a year, finished in 1967 for $6 million, and paid for by the North Stars' owners.

That parking lot was more important in promoting our first major league soccer team, the Kicks, in the 1970s than the mysterious action taking place inside on Met Stadium's grass and dirt. The first few Kicks summers included free parking, and oh, if

< 185 >

that asphalt could only have chronicled the debauched scenes it hosted—a steamy best seller for sure.

The Minneapolis Lakers left Minnesota in 1960, the lack of an adequate arena being an excuse and Bob Short's desire for the big money market of LA being the reason. It was nearly three decades before the NBA returned with the expansion Timberwolves in 1989. That first season, the owners, Marv Wolfenson and Harvey Ratner, rented dates in the Metrodome (where they set an NBA attendance record), and then they moved the team into a building they paid for themselves.

That broke 'em as owners, and then Glen Taylor saved the franchise, and Target Center has now been thoroughly remodeled. Go ahead and wonder how long that will be satisfactory to newest owners Marc Lore and Alex Rodriguez.

Pro championships have been celebrated in that building— provided by the Lynx, our WNBA team.

The first arena to show us that substantial public assistance could be reasonably painless was Xcel Energy Center, which opened in the fall of 2000. The "X" served the joint purpose of bringing the NHL back to Minnesota with the expansion Wild and bringing life to downtown St. Paul for nearly 50 nights—starting in late September and generally ending in the sixth game of the first round of the playoffs.

And since the X, we gave the Gophers a new on-campus football stadium in 2009, the Twins the picturesque Target Field in 2010, and the Vikings the over-the-top, $1.15 billion U.S. Bank Stadium in 2016—all in Minneapolis.

St. Paul followed the X with CHS Field, a $65 million minor league ballpark for the Saints. Saints mogul Mike Veeck getting that ballpark built in Lowertown might be the biggest Minnesota sports upset of my lifetime.

The frosting on the St. Paul sports cake is Allianz Field, which was funded privately in the Midway arena. This is the spectacular home to Minnesota United FC of Major League Soccer. Unlike a Kicks crowd, these fans like to come inside. They even sing about it.

Minnesotans can complain more than ever about sports, with online platforms so plentiful that Twitter is now for us old people. Whether we're seething on our couches at home or sitting in overpriced seats at the arena, we can just pull out our phones and threaten to disown our teams for too many false starts, bad pitching, or a perceived political bent with which we don't agree.

Yet we have never been so invested in sports and never had it so readily available (as long as you subscribe to the right TV outlets). When the Twins arrived in 1961, four home games and one-third of the road games were shown on television each season. Now we can't understand why a meaningless Summer League game for the Timberwolves had to be shown on tape delay.

In 1997 I wrote Sid Hartman's biography, and it was filled with tales of delivering a check to buy the Detroit Gems and turning them into the dynastic Lakers; working through the '50s to bring big-league baseball here and succeeding in October 1960; Sid's involvement in landing the expansion Vikings for 1961; and other triumphs as Sid and the Minneapolis power brokers battled to make us major league.

None of that for you here. I can tell some stories about determinedly making last call at Luigi's in St. Paul with Gregg Wong, Carl Peterson, Jim Wells, and other *Pioneer Press* colleagues; of Glen Sonmor and me being the guest speakers at the Nativity Church men's club and embarrassing several monsignors with bawdy language; or of Mike Augustin and me finding ourselves in North Stars coach Wren Blair's Met Center office at 2 AM after a playoff game and him quizzing us guys from Springfield and Fulda, as if we knew something about hockey.

And here's one you would never get from Sid: the real reason the Twins came back from being down three games to two to win their first World Series in 1987.

Wayne Hattaway had been a clubhouse attendant for all those

players on the '87 squad who came up through the Twins' minor leagues. And all the new guys met him during spring training. Hattaway's nickname was "Big Fella," because that's how he addressed everyone—such as seeing a reporter (me) at spring training and every year saying, "Hey, big fella, you got even fatter this winter."

Big Fella said he was in charge of telling Twins players "how good they ain't."

The Twins flew Hattaway in to Minneapolis from Orlando for Game 6 of the series after three losses in St. Louis had seemed to turn the World Series to the Cardinals.

The Twins players were all stretching out in left field around 4 PM, a few hours before the game was set to start. Who knows what level of mental tightness was with this bunch? Whatever it was, it would soon disappear.

Hattaway came charging out from the dugout toward the team stretch. He was wearing a red duster and his goofy grin.

"I knew you guys were going to choke," Big Fella said. "I knew you couldn't handle the pressure. You won the first two games, and I told everybody in Orlando: 'They're going to choke. They'll lose the next four.'"

Laughter erupted from the players. Insults were hurled back toward Big Fella. He had managed to loosen whatever tension there had been.

I'm telling you, right here, right now, the Homer Hankies might have helped the '87 Twins get those last two wins in the Dome, but the key inspiration was Hattaway showing up to tell the Twins how good they ain't.

ACKNOWLEDGMENTS

I would like to acknowledge my wife, Katy, for accepting the fact she was married to someone who did not have the handyman skills to change a light bulb and, thus, for handling automatically all home matters inside or out for more than 30 years.

—Patrick Reusse

I have been *Star Tribune* teammates with Patrick Reusse since January 2000. When I mentioned I had an idea I wanted to run past him, we met at Gopher Bar in St. Paul for coney dogs.

I'm grateful he said yes to my idea about this book. Listening to Patrick share stories about his remarkable life and career was a thrill. There is no better storyteller, and to get a front-row seat to hours of Reusse's hilarious memories was a true gift I won't ever forget.

Two people encouraged my love of writing and supported my ambition to be a sportswriter more than anyone else: my mom, Judy, and my dad, Ken. My dad died in 2017, and my mom passed away while I was writing this book. I wish they were here to read it, but I know they are proud.

Finally, this book and my writing career would not be possible without the love and never-ending support I receive from my wife, Amy, and children, Megan, Spencer, and Joe. They are the MVPs. This book is for them and for making me feel like the luckiest man on Earth.

—Chip Scoggins

< 189 >

INDEX

ABOUT THE AUTHORS

Patrick Reusse spent his first 16 years in Fulda, a town of 1,100 residents in southwest Minnesota. His father, Richard, and older brother, Michael, demonstrated to Patrick that a passion for sports was best served with a touch of irreverence.

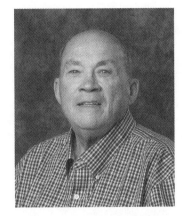

After Patrick's mother, Cecile, died in 1962, the family of four, including younger sister Meg, moved to Prior Lake, where Patrick graduated from high school in 1963. Late that summer, he landed a part-time job as a copy boy in the sports department at the *Minneapolis Morning Tribune.*

From the first night amidst the *Tribune*'s cast of characters—including sports editor Sid Hartman—Reusse wanted a career working in sports departments. He went on to do just that in Duluth, St. Cloud, St. Paul, and, since 1988, as a sports columnist at the Minneapolis *Star Tribune.*

Reusse and his wife, Kathleen Dillon, have lived in the same home in Golden Valley since 1988. He has three sons (James Reusse, Chris Reusse, and Ryan Dillon), two daughters-in-law (Edna Reusse and Carrie Dillon), and two grandkids entering teenage years, Abby and Luke Dillon.

Chip Scoggins is an award-winning sportswriter for the Minneapolis *Star Tribune.* A three-time winner of Minnesota's sportswriter of the year award, Scoggins has worked for the *Star Tribune* since 2000 in a variety of roles. He became a sports columnist and features writer in 2011. His work has been honored by the Associated Press Sports Editors, National Sports Media Association, and Society of Professional Journalists.

Scoggins previously worked for newspapers in Missouri, Texas, Connecticut, North Carolina, and Illinois. He is married with three children and lives in Woodbury, Minnesota.